PROVISION

*Releasing Supernatural
Increase in Your Life*

LAWSON PERDUE

Provision: Releasing Supernatural Increase in Your Life
ISBN: 979-8-7508949-9-4
Copyright © 2021 by Lawson Perdue

Cover Design by Joanie Kanneberg
D'Armond Designs

For more information, please visit
CharisChristianCenter.com

For ease of understanding, unless otherwise
noted, all scriptures are the author's paraphrase
of the *King James Version* of the Bible (1611,
Public Domain).

Charis
CHRISTIAN CENTER

CharisChristianCenter.com
10285 Federal Drive
Colorado Springs, CO 80908
719.227.0380

TABLE OF CONTENTS

FOREWORD

I first met Lawson Perdue when he was fourteen years old. His mother bribed him to come to a Bible Study I was teaching in Lamar, Colorado by offering to supply him with some fish bait if he would go. The Lord touched him that night and Lawson received the baptism of the Holy Spirit and a call to preach. He has been passionately seeking the Lord ever since.

Lawson has a tremendous revelation of the true Gospel and is sharing it through pastoring a church that he started with only his family and one other couple. He is on international daily television, has written eight books, and has many teaching series on a wide range of topics. He's also one of the favorite teachers at our Charis Bible College.

But one of the greatest revelations I see in Lawson and Barbara is their understanding of how prosperity works. They have exercised this in their personal lives since the beginning, never totally depending on the ministry alone to supply their needs.

They have wisely had multiple streams of income, which has allowed them to prosper much more than what most pastors experience. Their three boys had this modeled to them, and these same values are prospering their families too.

Lawson moved in to their current 120,000 sq. ft. facility, with all the renovations done debt free, on their very first Sunday. That's very rare in Christianity today. This debt-free living allows Lawson and Barbara to put more money into the Gospel.

Although I'm not aware of all of their giving, I know Charis Christian Center has put hundreds of thousands of dollars into my ministry and our Charis Bible College. And I know they support many other ministries and missionaries around the world. They are strong givers, and it shows.

These things haven't happened just sovereignly or by chance. The Word of God teaches us to prosper and guarantees success if we don't depart from its instruction (Joshua 1:8). Lawson has learned these truths and desires to impart to you what has worked for him. God is no respecter of persons (Romans 2:11). What has worked for Lawson and Barbara will work for you too.

Open your heart and get ready to receive revelation that will change your life.

Andrew Wommack
President and Founder of Charis Bible College
and Andrew Wommack Ministries

A SPECIAL MESSAGE

FROM

DR. JESSE DUPLANTIS

It's my joy to recommend to you *Provision: Releasing Supernatural Increase in Your Life* by Lawson Perdue. I can tell you firsthand that Lawson knows what he's doing and what he's talking about in this book because it's working in his life.

It's working in my life, too. The anointing of increase is greatly on my life—spiritually, physically, financially, in every area—and I tell people all the time that it can't just be on one person; it has to be on the whole body of Christ.

As Lawson says, these are not hypothetical ideas but practical truths of the scripture that will change your life and anyone else you get around, if you believe them.

I know you're going to be blessed by this book. And I want you to read it not just once, but again and again until it becomes a living reality in your innermost being.

Because, you see, you can't have what you

preach against. If you're against prosperity, you'll never be prosperous. If you're against healing, you'll never be healed. But if you believe what God says, and not what people say, you'll have that anointing of increase all over you every day of your life. No matter how bad it is out there, what's inside of you is greater than anything you can see!

So, sit down and enjoy this book... It is going to change your life. It has changed mine! I've read some things in here that have already ministered to me, and I'm bubbling up on the inside. Remember that increase is for *you*—not for the devil, and not for the devil's crowd—and Lawson Perdue will show you how.

You have to receive this message and know without a shadow of doubt that *God wants you to prosper.* It's all over the Bible! Friend, your prosperity starts with you the day you start reading this book!

Dr. Jesse Duplantis
Evangelist, Author, TV Host
President and Founder of
Jesse Duplantis Ministries

ENDORSEMENT

Provision contains the words of a father and pastor whose heart wants you to prosper, and whose wisdom can help you have a great and prosperous future. This book is a roadmap for you to walk onto the road of prosperity.

Pastor Lawson is a father, and, as a father, he wants his children to prosper. He taught all his sons to prosper, and they all have. As a pastor, he wants his sheep to prosper as well in all areas of their lives.

I have known many over the years who sit in the same chairs I do every Sunday. They have applied the principles you are about to read and have seen an abundance of prosperity in their lives.

I have seen many people more than double financially. Since meeting Pastor Lawson, I have personally almost tripled my annual income.

One of the key principles in the book *Provision* is believing. As you read these pages, my prayer would be that your heart believes the words this father and pastor is sharing with you. These truths are biblical principles but must be believed for them to manifest in your life.

I encourage you to read and believe, create your plan and your team, and enter God's greatest life for you and your family.

Dr. Doug Weiss
Licensed Psychologist
and Executive Director of
Heart to Heart Counseling Center

INTRODUCTION

God has made many promises to His children. In addition to the promises of redemption for forgiveness of sin, peace of mind, and healing of the body, there are many promises of financial provision in the Word of God as well.

God made provision for humanity in Jesus Christ, and we can receive that provision through faith. This book is about accessing the grace of God revealed in Christ, specifically in the area of financial provision, by faith.

Just like we as believers access the promises of God in any other area of redemption, we can access the promise of God concerning financial provision. This is not a book of hypothetical ideas, but of practical truths of the scriptures that have changed my life and the lives of many others who also believe them.

It's my desire that as people see and hear these practical truths of the Bible, they will be encouraged in their faith, able to put into practice these practical principles, and see supernatural increase released in their lives.

Chapter
One

GOD WANTS YOU
TO PROSPER

The first major revelation I ever had in the area of finances was that God *wants* us to prosper. He wants us to prosper spiritually, emotionally, physically, and financially. It is His Nature, His Promise, His Provision.

3 John 2

"peri"
concerning all things

<u>Beloved</u> *I wish above all things, that you would prosper and be in health even as your soul prospers.*

The Greek word for prosper in 3 John 2 is *eudoo*. It means to help along the way. We all need some help between here and heaven!

Successful journey

This word carries the essence of a Father to His children. I have three sons. I want them to prosper. So, as I have raised them, I have given them some help along the way.

3

All three of my sons are doing well, both spiritually and financially. Several things have played a role in this. Most importantly, they are all believers. They are intelligent and use critical thinking skills. They all have a great work ethics and good attitudes. Each one of them are prospering, primarily because they all know that God *wants* them to prosper.

This word, *eudoo*, also has the connotation of a pastor to his flock. I want my congregation to prosper. I have seen many people over the years come to the church, get ahold of the truth of the Word of God, and begin to prosper more and more. I believe this is the will of God for every believer.

God Is More than Enough

Genesis 17:1-2

> *And when Abram was ninety-nine years old, the LORD appeared to Abram, and said unto him, I am the Almighty God; walk before me and be perfect. And I will make my covenant between me and. you, and will multiply you exceedingly.*

God appeared to Abram when he was ninety-nine years old and revealed Himself as the Almighty God. This Word in the Hebrew is the Word *El Shaddai*. It means the All-Sufficient God, who is more than enough: the many-breasted God. He has so much sufficiency running out of Him, we don't even have room enough to consume it.

God spoke to Abraham and said, "Walk before me and be perfect, and I will multiply you exceedingly." When we come into a relationship with God and understand who He really is, we will begin to see who He is magnified in our lives. He is More than Enough, and believing this is key to seeing His Sufficiency revealed.

In Genesis 17, as God conversed with Abram, He told him that he was to change his name to Abraham. Abram means fatherly. Abraham means father of many nations.

Abraham had to have a change of identity to have a change of destiny.

As long as we continue to identify with poverty, we will not have the abundance of God revealed in our lives to the level that God wants to make it known to us. For years, the church has struggled with a poverty mentality. Even to a point of equating poverty with holiness. The scripture teaches no such thing.

We need to see ourselves how God sees us so we can possess what God wants us to possess. We need to quit identifying with poverty. We need to quit speaking lack and insufficiency and begin to speak provision and sufficiency. Our God is more than enough! + extra

I have made this my confession for years, "I have everything I need to do everything God has called me to do, and I have no lack in any area of my life." I am seeing that become reality more and more. This does not mean that I don't ever need

5

to believe God for provision. It means, however, that I have chosen to put my eyes on God and His sufficiency rather than on the lack and insufficiency of this world.

Many times, the world is focusing on lack, even where there truly is none. In the 1970's, there was a supposed oil shortage. My uncle was working in the oil field during this time in Southeastern Colorado. They were drilling good wells and capping them. There was *plenty* of supply. They just were giving people false information, so there was a false sense of lack.

There are basically two mentalities in life. One is, "There is more where that came from." The other is, "There is not enough." But the truth is, as long as humanity is on planet Earth, there will be enough provision for them.

Genesis 8:22

> *While the earth remains, seedtime and harvest, and cold and heat, summer and winter, and day and night shall not cease.*

We have been lied to. Many people are worried about global warming, running out of food, or whatever other calamities they can dream up.

During the recent Covid crisis, people were acting crazy, buying up everything, including toilet paper. For a while it was hard to find these things on the shelves in the stores.

During this time, my wife Barbara and I went to the local grocery store. We bought some fruit and veggies and a couple other small things. Many of the store's shelves were bare in the canned goods areas, and others. People had shopping carts full of non-perishables.

We left the store with only a few perishable items. One lady noticed it and said, "You aren't from here, are you?" My wife told her that I was raised on the farm, and being raised on the farm, I knew there would always be enough.

When we know who God really is, we know there will always be more than enough.

God is Our Provider

In Genesis 22, God spoke to Abraham and told him to take Isaac, his son, and offer him in the place that He would show him. Abraham took a three-day journey to Moriah and found the place God had revealed to him. He proceeded to take Isaac and prepared for the offering.

Just before doing the unthinkable, the angel of the Lord stayed Abraham's hand with a shout. When Abraham looked, he saw a ram caught in a thicket by his horns.

Genesis 22:13-14

Abraham lifted up his eyes, and looked, and behold behind him a ram caught in a thicket by his horns: and Abraham

*went and took the ram, and offered him
up for a burnt offering in the place of his
son. And Abraham called the name of
that place Jehovah-Jireh: as it is said to
this day, In the mount of the* LORD *it shall
be seen.*

God is Jehovah-Jireh. He is the Lord our
provider. Thank God: When we know that God is
our provider, we don't need to fear lack.

I believe Abraham looked at Calvary, just a few
hundred yards north of Moriah, and saw the ram.
He then took the ram and offered him in the place
of his son. Then he called the name of the place
Jehovah-Jireh. This means, "in the mount of the
Lord it shall be seen; God is my provider."

In John 8:56, Jesus said, "*Your father
Abraham rejoiced to see My day, and He saw and
was glad.*"

Abraham rejoiced when he saw the provision
of God. I believe he received a revelation of the
future redemption coming in Christ.

In Christ God provided everything we would
ever need. He provided righteousness for our sin,
peace for our anxiety, healing for our sickness
and provision for our poverty. There is provision
in the cross of Jesus Christ (Isaiah 53:4-5, 2
Corinthians 8:9). He has taken care of it all!

Just like Jesus was wounded for our transgressions and bruised for our iniquities, and just
as He took stripes on His back for our healing, He

also took our poverty. At the same time Jesus died and took our sins, our anxiety, and our sickness. Jesus took our poverty.

I heard Dr. Lester Sumrall say one time, "I hate sickness like I hate sin, because it comes from the same place." That, my friends, is the Gospel truth. But I would like to add to that statement: "I hate poverty like I hate sin, because it comes from the same place."

2 Cor 4:3-4   unbelievers + even believers

The devil has tried to keep the church spiritually (blind) to the Gospel truth of healing and provision. I think the devil wants to keep the body of Christ sick and poor. It is hard for us to get much accomplished in the world if we are too sick and too poor to do what God has called us to do.

We need to wake up to the biblical fact that God wants us to be healthy and prosperous (3 John 2). We need to wake up to the fact that God is our provider, and Jesus made provision a reality through His death, burial, and resurrection.

Chapter Two

HUMBLE BEGINNINGS

I grew up in a traditional church. I received Christ at the young age of eight and was saved. However, in the church I grew up in, they never taught people the biblical truth that God wants us to prosper. In fact, they nearly equated poverty with holiness! Nothing could be further from the truth.

Poverty is not holiness, nor will it make you holy. Financial prosperity is not holiness. Money cannot make you holy, but the lack of money can't do that either. Only the blood of Jesus can make a person whole and holy.

I can hear someone thinking, *But I thought money is the root of all evil.* Money is *not* the root of all evil. The *love of money* is the root of all evil! You can love money and not have a dime.

Money is just a tool. It is indifferent. If you give money to a good man, he will do good things with it. If you give money to an evil man, he will do evil things with it.

When I was fourteen years old, I went to a Bible study taught by Andrew Wommack. My mother promised me that she would buy me some fish bait if I went to the Bible study with her. We lived in the country, and I loved fishing, so I took my mom up on her offer. True to her word, she took me to Kmart before the Bible study and bought me some fish bait.

But that night something happened. I heard the Bible preached in a whole different light than I had ever heard it preached before.

I remember sitting on the floor. The living room in the home Bible study was so full of people that I chose to sit on the floor to make room for others. When Andrew picked up his Bible to teach, the Holy Spirit spoke to me and said, "Listen to this man; he knows what he is talking about." I was all ears.

That night, this truth came to me: *I don't have to be sick, poor and defeated by the devil. There is a Bible full of promises that I can believe.* I started believing God, and the scriptures took on a whole new meaning in my life.

The Gospel created hope in my life. My parents had always struggled financially. My dad had a major physical nervous condition that hindered him financially and created some problems in my parent's marriage.

But from that day, things began to get better in my life. The Word of God began to create a picture in me of health and prosperity. I began to see life differently. I began to believe that I could provide well for my family and that I could have a successful life in the area of finances. I also began to believe that I could live healthy and strong. The Word of God began to change my mind and thereby change my life.

The year was 1978. I began to believe that I could have a hundred-thousand-dollar net worth and make a living. But it didn't stop there. There has been a continual growth in the area of financial increase throughout my life since that day. I am far beyond that stage today, and I don't believe that God is done yet!

However, this truth came to me and has stayed with me. It is the truth of the Gospel, revealed again and again in the scripture. God wants us to prosper.

Consider these scriptures:

Psalm 35:27 (NKJV)

> *...And let them say continually, "Let the LORD be magnified, Who has pleasure in the prosperity of His servant."*

Philippians 4:19

> *But my God shall supply all your need according to His riches in glory by Christ Jesus.*

We will have many more scriptures to consider in this book. It has been said that there are over two thousand scriptures in the Bible that talk about money, wealth and riches. It is about time we get a biblical perspective instead of a religious perspective.

Religion will keep people poor and sick and hinder them from accomplishing the plan and purpose of God in their lives.

Chapter
Three

BELIEVING

A few years back, I was teaching in Florida and people begin to ask me questions concerning financial prosperity. As I answered the questions, this teaching came to me. There are four pillars, or main truths, to financial success: Believing, Giving, Stewardship and Work.

Believing

Isaiah 7:9

> ...If you will not believe, surely you shall not be established.

What we believe has a lot to do with what we receive. Sad to say, many in the church do not believe that God wants them to prosper. Recently, a man from another church was talking to my oldest son, Aaron, about healing. As they spoke, this man began to see the truth of the scripture concerning divine healing. Gaining this new revelation made him want to teach a Bible study in his church about healing.

However, when he went to the elders in his church and asked, they said, "Don't tell anyone, but we are cessationists. We believe that healing ceased with the apostles in the Bible."

Aaron then invited the man to come to our church. He responded, "I cannot come to your church because of what you believe about prosperity." Sadly, this is the thinking of many in the Body of Christ.

I have a missionary friend to whom I had given some money because he does a lot of good work. However, he is from a different group of believers. One day, he sent an email criticizing "prosperity preachers."

I sent him a reply. I told him that he could not live where he lived without prosperity. He lives in a nice house in a beautiful city. I told him that he could not help the people who he helps without prosperity. I told him that he needs prosperity to do what God has called him to do, and then I sent him a list of about fifty scriptures proving the will of God concerning prosperity!

That was a few years ago, and thank God, I have never heard of him criticizing prosperity preachers again. I recently liked one of his newsletters and sent him another offering. He really does a lot of good work in the kingdom, and I hope to support him more in the future.

It is time we get back to preaching what the Bible says instead of a bunch of doctrines of men that keep people from receiving the promises of

God. If we don't get our believing straightened out, we will have problems in the area of receiving! What you believe is paramount for what you receive.

I've been believing well for a long time, and it is positively affecting what I receive. In February of 1988, when I was attending Bible School at Dr. Lester Sumrall's school in South Bend, Indiana, they invited a guest to speak on Sunday morning. The speaker said, "How many people here are believing for a million dollars? Stand up!"

I remember it vividly. There were about 3000 people in attendance that morning, and three of us (including me) stood up. I thought, *How pathetic. We want to preach the Gospel and change the world, but only three in three thousand are believing for a million dollars.*

I don't know who the other two people were, but I reached that goal in my life a number of years back.

Understand this: believing is not about your current circumstances. It is about your thinking.

Barbara, Aaron, and I were living in Mr. Gilmer's house in Gilmer Park on Gilmer Street. Mr. Gilmer lived in that house in the 1800's with an Indian bride. It was a shack. I was making a little over four dollars per hour working for Dr. Sumrall, and I was attending Bible School at night. But it did not hinder my believing.

Even though our family had humble beginnings, we believed what the Word of God says about the blessing and favor of God. Barbara and I knew that if God said it, it would come to pass! So, we kept believing, and we have increased steadily over the years.

I have learned how to believe God not only personally, but in the church. In the year 2001, God spoke to me and told me to move to Colorado Springs and start a church, Charis Christian Center. Barbara actually had some direction to that prior to me, so she began preparing ahead of time.

Even though God had spoken to me, it wasn't easy in the beginning. We held Bible studies in Colorado Springs for six months prior to officially launching the church.

Our first Bible study was held in a home the first Thursday night of March in the Mountain Shadows area of Colorado Springs. Greg Troup rented a room at that home. He had grown up in our church in Kit Carson and had told me prior to coming to Colorado Springs that if I would start a church within sixty miles, he would come. So, we took him up on the offer. We then officially launched the church, Charis Christian Center, on September 10, 2001, the day before 9-11.

Some Sundays there wasn't even $100 total in the offering, and $50 of it was our personal giving. That is when faith kicked in. I began to believe for $5000 per month. When we reached that goal, I started believing for $10,000 per month; then $250,000 per year; then $500,000 per year; then $1 million per year; then $2 million per year; then

$3 million per year. Right now, as I write these words, I am believing for $7 million dollars per year. I have long term goals far beyond these!

Jesse Duplantis came and spoke for our 10th anniversary. We were at $1,000,000 per year then. He kept telling me to "Believe God; Believe God; Believe God." I had written a thank you note and included an offering from our church to his ministry. I asked him if he wanted it before the meeting or after.

He said, "I'll take it now." He opened it and said, "My Goodness, you *are* believing God!"

When I took him back to his jet to leave the next day, he took Barbara and I with him to show us the jet. I told him that I was believing God then for $2 million per year and for $10 million per year, long term.

He said, "When you get there, don't stop! We should never stop in our pursuit of believing God."

It is never too early to start believing God, regardless of age or circumstance. Believe the promises of the Bible. All of the promises of God in Christ are "Yes" and "Amen," to the glory of God by us (2 Corinthians 1:20). All of the promises are for us. God wants us saved, healed, and blessed! But we must believe it to receive it.

Chapter

Four

GIVING

G iving is the second pillar of financial
success. There are multiple types of
giving—tithing, offering, and alms—and
all can be considered planting seed!

Luke 6:38

> Give, and it shall be given to you, good
> measure, pressed down, and shaken
> together, and running over, shall men
> give into your bosom. For with the same
> measure that you measure, it shall be
> measured to you again.

When I was about four years old, my dad gave
me two nickels to put in the Sunday School
offering. I put one in, but I kept one because I
wanted some bubble gum. When we were going
home that day, I asked my dad to stop at the store
in town to buy some bubble gum.

Dad said, "I don't have money for bubble gum."
He talked about being poor as Job's turkey, and
we kind of lived that way. (But maybe Job's

turkey was rich! Job was the wealthiest of the men of the East before the devil attacked him, and at the end of the book he received back twice what he had previously.)

Anyway, when we were about to the country store, three miles before our house, I asked my dad to stop again to get some bubble gum. He repeated, "I don't have money for bubble gum."

I then replied, "But I have a nickel."

Immediately realizing what had happened, my dad asked, "Son, did you keep one of the nickels that I gave you for Sunday School"

"Yes, Daddy," I admitted.

My dad went on to teach me an important spiritual truth. He said, "Son, we give ten percent of everything (the tithe) to God." I still remember that. I remember when I was thirteen years old, tithing from my summer paycheck for driving tractor to my Sunday School class. That tithe was over $130.

Because my dad taught me that truth as a child, I have always been a tither. I have always faithfully paid my bills. I have never been without. Some of the time, things may have been challenging, but all of my needs were met.

It is interesting. Even though my dad had some not-so-holy habits (cussing, smoking and drinking), he always insisted that we tithe and go to church.

Tithing and attending church have served me well. I had some not-so-holy habits of my own, but when I received a revelation of grace, it really helped me in those areas!

There are three major areas of giving spoken of in the Bible: tithing, offering, and alms. Tithing is giving the first ten percent of your income to God. I like to tithe to the storehouse where I am getting fed. Optimally, that is a good, life-giving church where the truths of the Bible are taught and people are being saved, healed, and set free.

Offering is giving above and beyond the tithe. It is a gift of our will, where we see fit, to any life-giving ministry. Alms giving is giving to the poor. I give in all of these areas.

However, I want to talk about a principle in the area of giving that I believe supersedes all of them. This is the area of sowing seed.

Even though tithing, offering and alms are major areas of giving revealed in the scripture, I like to give everything I give as a seed. If I give it as a seed, it has a future. Seed produces harvest.

In 2 Corinthians 8-9, Paul addresses the area of financial responsibility and financial increase in the church. The major thing he focuses on is seed sowing. He also speaks of the grace of giving.

Interestingly, the only other place in scripture that talks about grace as much as 2 Corinthians 8-9 is Romans 5-6, where Paul talks about righteousness.

23

Provision

Every believer needs to get involved in the grace of giving. When you begin to get revelation in this area and are consistent in it, I believe you are begin to enter into a realm of harvest like never before.

As I said before, I operate in all of the major areas of giving: tithing, offering and alms. But again, I see it all as seed! I grew up on a farm, so I know a little something about seed. If you want to get a good harvest you must sow your seed in good soil.

I also look at my giving as an investment. When I invest money, I like to invest in things that have explosive growth potential. In other words, I like to invest where I will get a good return. It's the same way in the body of Christ. I give money to some really prosperous ministries. I believe I have a good return on my investment.

All this being said, I am a tither. I give to the poor, and I give offerings. I personally give much more than ten percent of my income. This is only possible because God has been good to me.

I heard this saying from Kenneth E. Hagin, and I believe it will help you: *I am a tither; I am a giver; I do not lack ability; I do not lack opportunity and I will never lack for money!*

I have added my own personal confession: *I have everything I need to do everything God called me to do; I have no lack in any area of my life. I am blessed and highly favored of the Lord!*

Get involved in the grace of giving; it will release all grace to you! God is able to make all grace abound to you that you always having all sufficiency in all things may abound to every good work (2 Corinthians 9:8).

Chapter *Five*

STEWARDSHIP

Stewardship is the third major area of financial success, and it can be summed up with the following statement:

✗ If your outgo exceeds your income, your upkeep will be your downfall.

1 Corinthians 4:1

> So let a man think of us as ministers of Christ and stewards of the mysteries of God.

Luke 16:10-12 (NKJV)

> He who is faithful in what is least is faithful also in much; and he who is unjust in what is least is unjust also in much. Therefore if you have not been faithful in the unrighteous mammon, who will commit to your trust the true riches? And if you have not been faithful in what is another man's, who will give you what is your own?

We need to be stewards of our time, our talents, and our treasure. The way we handle money (that which is least) will determine how we handle spiritual things (that which is much). If we have not been faithful in money, we will not be faithful in spiritual things.

Over the years, there have been many books written concerning financial stewardship. I believe there are some very good resources for people in this area. I am not going to try to re-create those in this book. However, I am going to mention a few principles that will help believers get to the next level of financial prosperity.

Years ago, in the late 1980's and early 1990's, I read a number of Christian books concerning the area of stewardship. As I would try to fill in all the blanks concerning a budget, I would get frustrated. The reason it was frustrating was because I didn't have enough income to fill in all the blanks! In my frustration, God would speak to me and tell me that He was taking care of me.

Then in 1994, I received my second major revelation in the area of finances. I remember it so well, because people had told me that when I had been married for ten years, my financial circumstances would be better.

Barbara and I, with several families from the area, had planted a church in Kit Carson, Colorado, Church of the Redeemed, in 1988. It was a very special group of people and a very special time in our life. We have many lifelong friends from those years.

On our tenth wedding anniversary, May 19, 1994, Barbara and I, and our three sons, Aaron, Andrew, and Peter, traveled to Colorado Springs to celebrate. We went to the dollar theater—you could go to a movie for a dollar—then to a cafeteria for lunch, and on to WalMart for supplies before heading back to Kit Carson.

On the way home, I stopped at the post office to pick up the mail, and the transmission went out in our Chevy van. I remember it so well because I had just put tires on the van and already owed the local Texaco owner $400 for the tires!

So, people had told me, "It will be better when you have been married for ten years." But on our ten-year anniversary, the used transmission we found for the van cost $800. I also owed the local grocery store about $300 for groceries. So, as of that day, I had about $1500 of consumer debt!

But something was about to change. The next day, I went to my church office, and I went through a workbook on financial stewardship and increase by Patrick Ondery and John Avanzini. Something about this book was different. They said, "Some of you have cut back all you can cut back, and you need to believe God for specific amounts of increase!"

This was the second major revelation that I personally received in the area of finances. You can believe God for specific amounts of money.

I did the budget, saw the shortfall, and I started believing for a specific amount of money.

I started believing for $1500 immediately to get rid of my consumer debt, and I started believing for an increase of $700 per month to fill in all the blanks in the budget.

Believe me, I know how to make a dollar stretch! One of my elders once told me, "Pastor, you don't only get Lincoln's face off of the front of the penny, you get the memorial off of the back, too!"

My grandparents went through the Great Depression in the 1930's. They had major influence in my life, and my grandmother Ruby saved everything. Before you went out and bought something, you went out to the barn, or the junk pile, or the grove of trees, or a granary, or a storage building to see if you could find it first!

Remember, if your outgo exceeds your income, your upkeep will be your downfall.

Now, I started believing for $1500 to pay my immediate bills on May 20, 1984. By June 6, 1984, I received the $1500, and I paid all of my immediate bills.

I hadn't told anyone about my need. I just prayed and thanked God for the need being met. I remember that different people came and gave me money. None of them were from my church. Some of them had never given me money before. One minister friend drove over sixty miles and gave me $100. He had never given me money before, and he has never given money to me since. But he heard God and gave.

Faith can bring money to you. Not only did I receive that $1500 and have my immediate needs met, within one year's time I had the $700 per month increase, so that I could live better without such struggle. That was an important revelation for me, and it has changed my life.

When I read that workbook, I thought, *This is easy. I have faith. I can believe God.* I knew that I could believe God for peace. I knew that I could believe God for health, and then I got the revelation that I can believe God for specific amounts of money!

Faith is a Journey

After we had been in Colorado Springs for about a year, I was walking around Bear Creek Park in the summer and asking God where our building would be. I heard His voice clearly, "Faith is a journey; enjoy the trip."

In 2003, Andrew Wommack was in the build out process of his new ministry headquarters on Elkton Drive. God told me to give him a large gift at that point in time for his ministry. In fact, He instructed me two weeks prior the amount and specific day I was to give it.

I wrote the check the day God spoke to me and put it in a card. I wrote a message, thanking Andrew and Jamie for everything they had done for us and added that I was grateful to be a part of Charis Bible College. I sealed it and put it on a dresser in my bedroom until the appointed time.

The day I gave it to Andrew, he just took the envelope. He didn't open it or look at the amount. He didn't read the note. He then told me that he wanted me to have my church services in his building on Elkton Drive! That was a tremendous blessing and helped establish Charis Christian Center in Colorado Springs.

The 10/10/80 Plan

Believing, giving, and stewardship all are part of the process for lasting financial increase. In the realm of stewardship, I think everyone needs a basic plan. I like to live by the 10/10/80 plan.

In this plan, you *give* the first 10%, you *save* or *invest* the next 10%, and you discipline yourself to *live* on the remaining 80%. You can give more than 10%, but that needs to come out of the 80%.

I recently heard a teaching on devotional and transactional money. The speaker, who is a long-time friend, said that most preachers don't know what transactional money is. I completely agree and believe that this is good teaching.

There is money that we have which should be set aside for investment or business. This money is seed, intended for growth over time. If you eat your seed, you cannot grow a business, or have a harvest.

In the 10/10/80 plan, you try to keep your housing costs at or under 35% of your budget.

There may be a temporary change where a little more than 35% is used for housing, but over the long term it needs to be kept at 35%. This works for our natural house, and it will work for the church, our spiritual house, as well.

As pastors, Barbara and I have always given at least 10% of our ministry income to other ministries and missions. We started out with this goal while living and pastoring in Kit Carson. During our tenure at Church of the Redeemed, we gave about $50,000 per year to missions and other ministries. The church prospered and never lacked.

During our tenure here in Colorado Springs, we have given between 10 and 27% of the income of Charis Christian Center to missions and other ministries. I believe that this is one major key to our financial success.

We started Charis Christian Center in 2001 with almost no money and no people. As I write this book, we have about two-thousand people who consider CCC their church home. We have a building, valued at $22 million, completely paid for.

As a result of giving, and managing well what God has given us, we are preaching the Gospel across the United States and around the world. And we have money in investments for the next big opportunity God gives us to reach more people with the Gospel.

Here are a couple of other basic churches. First, always give at least life-giving ministries and missions programs which are outside of your control. Second, try to keep your personnel costs to 35% or less of your total income. Third, keep your long-term building costs to 35% or less of your total annual income. Fourth, invest for the future.

Dr. Lester Sumrall started a worldwide missions program called Feed the Hungry toward the end of his life. He also called it the end time Joseph program. Joseph lived by the principles that I am sharing. He saved one fifth of the harvest in the seven years of plenty.

One fifth equals 20%. What do you do with the first 20%? Give at least 10% and save or invest at least 10%. Discipline yourself to live off of 80% or less. If you do this for a long time, you will never regret it!

It works for our personal house and for our spiritual house, the church! Pastors, hear me. Give at least 10% of your church income to missions and other ministries outside of your control. Don't ask the people in your church to do what you will not do yourself. It will lead to major blessing!

In addition to giving, live on less than you make and do it for a long time. You will be amazed at the power of investment. Years ago, I watched Pat Robertson explain on a white board how quickly a person who makes $20,000 per year and spends $21,000 per year goes broke. Then he explained how quickly a person who makes $20,000 per year and spends $19,000 per year ts wealthy. And I have proved it really works.

Stewardship is a Biblical principle. If you don't believe it, read the book of Proverbs. Proverbs are just practical principles that work on the earth. They work for everyone, believer and unbeliever alike. Practice them and you will prosper!

Chapter
Six

WORK

Work is the fourth pillar (or principle) of financial success! Sometimes people argue with me about the subject of work. One person who used to come to our church told my son Aaron that he didn't believe in work. He felt that work was a curse. That is an absolute lie! Work is not a curse; it is a blessing!

At that time, Aaron was living in a house that had four bedrooms and three baths. He was a bachelor, so it was much bigger than he needed. That same man who told Aaron that work was a curse also told him that my son should let him, and his family, live in his house for free. Aaron explained to him that since he thought work was a curse, he could not come and live in Aaron's house because he worked to get the money to pay for the house!

Work is a scriptural principle. 2 Thessalonians 3:10 says that if a man does not work, neither should he eat. I think that was my dad's favorite scripture.

My dad worked for the forest service for about a year when he was first married and loved to plant trees. We planted hundreds of them on our farm in Southeastern Colorado. I remember toiling in the hot sun to water the trees and wash the dirt from them, but especially to cut all the weeds around them with a shovel. It would be over one hundred degrees and plenty humid on our irrigated farm in the summer. It was hateful work.

I told my dad one time that since Jesus was coming, we should not have to worry so much about planting trees and growing them. My dad replied, "The Bible says, 'Occupy till I come.' That means, get to work." My dad taught me young how to work, and the value of a dollar, and both lessons have served me well.

If you don't believe in work, you don't believe the Bible. God gave Adam, the first man, responsibility and authority. Today many people want authority without responsibility, but life doesn't work that way. God gave Adam a job before he gave him a wife.

Listen to me, young ladies. Let me give you some good advice. If you want to marry someone, first find someone who loves God more than he loves you (that's the only way he can love you enough). Find someone who is a giver and who likes to work. That will help you in life. Don't marry a lazy bum!

The people I know in the ministry—and out of it—who are really blessed are people who know how to work. I will name some ministry friends for you. If you follow them around, you will find out that they know how to work!

Dr. Lester Sumrall worked for about sixteen hours a day, getting up regularly at four or five in the morning every day. And that was after he went to bed around ten o'clock in the evening. I was told that it was only just before he went home to be with Jesus when he started taking a fifteen-minute power nap in the middle of the day.

Dr. Sumrall preached three hundred meetings a year outside of his own church and was in his own pulpit fifty out of fifty-two Sundays each year. He knew how to work. He loved his work. He loved God. He loved people. He spent his life preaching the Gospel and winning thousands of people to Christ around the world.

When I first met Andrew Wommack in 1978, he was holding six Bible Studies a week in Southeast Colorado and Western Kansas. The Bible studies were held on Monday through Saturday and started at seven o'clock in the evening.

Back in those days, those meetings would last until ten o'clock or later! Andrew then got up at four or five in the morning to record radio programs in a closet in his apartment. To this day, he still works circles around most people I know.

Jesse Duplantis worked as a young child in a grocery store. Later on, he worked as a rock musician. Jesse got saved and was offered a six-figure income to run a business on Wall Street, but he turned that down so he could fulfill his call in the ministry. Jesse Duplantis loves people. He loves sinners, and he works tirelessly to preach the Gospel.

Dr. Doug Weiss is another man who works very hard. I have known Dr. Weiss for about 10 years, and I consider him to be a very good friend. He regularly gets up at three to four in the morning. He has written over fifty books. He has helped people both in the church and outside of the church in marriage and life. He is high energy. He loves Jesus, he loves people, and he likes to work.

If anyone wants to make it in the ministry, they need to know the value of work. The Bible calls it the work of the ministry. The apostle Paul and my dad were right: If you don't work, you shouldn't eat. Quit griping about what you don't have, get a job, give to God first, and see what happens in life. You will experience the God who is more than enough!

Remember these four principles if you want to find and continue in financial success: believing, giving, stewardship and work. Don't blame someone else, or even God, for what you don't have. Start believing and activate the ability that God has given you and see His promises come to pass in your life.

Chapter
Seven

TAKING THE LIMITS
OF GOD

T he first major revelation that came to me in the way of financial prosperity is that God wants us to prosper. The second was that we can believe God for specific amounts of money. The third revelation that came to me is that we need to take the limits off of God.

Psalm 78:41-42

Yea, they turned back and tempted God, they limited the Holy One of Israel. They did not remember His hand, nor the day when He delivered them from the enemy.

Don't limit God, and don't forget what He has done for you!

In 1998, Pastor Billy Epperhart invited me and my family to attend meetings in Denver, Colorado where he had a number of guest speakers teaching. Pastor Billy put us up in a nice hotel for the week and paid for our meals. It was a tremendous blessing.

One of the speakers that week was Mark Hankins. Mark was teaching on double blessing from Isaiah 61:7. One of the examples he used really challenged my religious thinking in the area of financial increase.

Mark talked about buying his wife Trina a new luxury car. He said that he went to the local dealership where the dealer told him that the only way he could get the car he wanted was to go to another county, but that the one they had was on sale. Mark replied that he didn't want that model, he didn't want that color, and he didn't care if it was on sale.

This really challenged my limited thinking. I believed in "economize to evangelize." It seemed irresponsible to insist on such an expensive car when there was one readily available on sale. I really struggled with his example.

A One-French-Fry-Man

On Saturday, Barbara and I and our three sons, Aaron, Andrew and Peter headed home from the meeting.

We stopped by McDonalds to buy some lunch. Quarter pound cheeseburgers were the special: you could buy 2 for $2, or a meal for $3. So, I ordered one meal, four waters, and four quarter pound cheeseburgers for $7 plus tax.

I went to the restroom and returned to eat with the family, but I wasn't ready for what had happened in my absence. I got to the table to find my cheeseburger, a water, and the French fry box—with only *one* French fry.

"Where are my French fries?" I asked.

Barbara replied, "You can be a one-French-fry-man if you want to, but I believe that God has more!"

As we were driving home to Kit Carson, I discussed the topic, and Mark's example, with Barbara.

I remember her saying, "He is right, and you are wrong. You just need to get over it."

That Sunday morning, I got up and preached, not thinking much more about the conversation. Then early Monday morning, I went running.

God repeated Barbara's words to me, "He [Mark] was right, and you are wrong. You need to get over it."

I repented. I changed my thinking. Repentance doesn't only mean to change your actions; it can also mean to change your thinking. That change in my thinking led to major change in my life.

Had A Business

When I pastored in Kit Carson, I got into the cattle business on the side. Until that time, I had limited myself to a bank note of $100,000. When I realized I had been limiting God in my thinking, the next summer, I figured that I could borrow $500,000, buy a thousand head of cattle, and they would make money.

I didn't do that, but I did borrow $250,000 and bought around five or six hundred head of cattle, and they made good money. Later I borrowed up to $3 million on cattle and feed and had over three thousand head of cattle at one time. I made a lot more money than I lost. This is not always the case in the cattle business. Thank God for His grace.

Limitless in Ministry

Not only did my mind change in the area of business, but my mind changed in the area of ministry. While we pastored in Kit Carson, our church gave about $50,000 per year to missions and other ministries.

I began to think, *If I can pastor this church* (there were approximately 100 people who called it home) *and give $50,000 per year to missions and other ministries, I can pastor a church of a 1000 people and give away $500,000 per year to missions and other ministries.*

In 2016, that vision finally came to pass. Now I am believing for much more than that! This is one of the reasons that God blesses us. He blesses us so that we can be a blessing. God revealed this truth when He made covenant with Abraham in Genesis 12:1-3.

We are in covenant with God through Jesus Christ. All of His blessings are ours in Christ. God did not limit New Covenant blessings to only forgiveness of sins. Thank God, forgiveness, peace, healing, and prosperity are ours. Jesus paid for them at the cross (Isaiah 53:4-5, 1 Peter 2:24-25, 2 Corinthians 8:9).

The problem with many people in the church today is that we have limited God to only providing spiritual things. The promises of God are not only for spiritual things, but for emotional, physical, and financial things as well. We don't have to wait for heaven to live the good life. We can have a good life now and have heaven too (Deuteronomy 11:21).

Break Out of Small Thinking

We need to break out of small thinking and begin to expand our horizons. God is able to do exceedingly abundantly above all that we can ask or think according to the power that works in us (Ephesians 3:21).

If I hadn't accepted a new way of thinking, I would never have been able to move to Colorado Springs and start our church. I would have been limited to where I was. My business would have been limited, and my ministry would have been limited. This new way of thinking also affected my sons in a very positive way.

My three sons have done very well. When you break out of the box, it will help others around you to reach their potential.

My son Aaron went to Carnegie Mellon University and received his bachelor's degree, and then went on to Rice University to earn his master's and doctorate degrees. He started an online business and was making six figures a year, while full time in college, before coming to be my Associate Pastor.

My son Andrew graduated from Colorado School of Mines as the outstanding Chemical Engineering student with both his bachelor's and master's degrees. He now is part owner of a gas and oil engineering company and has given over six figures to his church at one time.

My son Peter graduated from Princeton University and now works for a division of the Three G Capital Company, Restaurant Brands International. Peter has most recently been named Vice President of Finance for Burger King of the Americas.

When I broke out of my little thinking, it helped my sons move more easily into the things that God had for them.

Every person is uniquely gifted by God. But when we see someone close to us move into their God-given destiny, I believe it helps us move into our God-given destiny as well.

Our believing affects our thinking. Our thinking affects our speaking. Our speaking affects our actions. And our actions affect our receiving. Change what you believe and change what you receive!

Chapter
Eight

THE BLESSING OF
THE LORD

God has blessed me immensely, both personally and in the ministry. Years ago, I was praying with Greg Fritz in our church in Kit Carson, and he told me that God was going to make me a millionaire.

Without the blessing of the Lord, Barbara and I would not be where we are personally, financially, or in the ministry.

There is only one way to really explain what has happened in our lives and ministry—it is supernatural. Without Jesus, what has happened for us would be impossible.

In this book, I am presenting some principles that lead to wealth. However, without Jesus in our lives, it just wouldn't be a reality!

Proverbs 10:22 (NKJV)

> *The blessing of the Lord makes one rich,*
> *And He adds no sorrow with it.*

When the Bible says that the blessing of the Lord makes rich, the Hebrew word for blessing is *berekah*. It is defined as blessings, prosperity, gift, or treaty of peace. The word for rich is *ashar*, which means to become rich or wealthy, to gain riches. *Esteb* is the word for sorrow, and it is defined as pain, toil, hurt, labor or hardship.

In other words, it is not what we have done or what we do that leads to the blessing of the Lord. It is the work He has done that leads us into blessing. Jesus did the work so that we can inherit the blessing.

There are three aspects of the blessing of the Lord that I want to address: the covenant of blessing, the priestly blessing, and the commanded blessing. These are all three Biblical principles of increase.

The Covenant of Blessing

Genesis 12:1-3

> *And Jehovah said to Abram, Go out of your country, and from your kindred, and from your father's house into a land that I will show you. And I will make you a great nation. And I will bless you and make your name great. And you shall be a blessing. And I will bless those that*

*bless you and curse the one who curses
you. And in you shall all families of the
earth be blessed.*

Abraham lived around 2000 BC. Before him,
there are only three times that it is recorded in scripture that God blessed humanity. They are found in
Genesis 1:28, Genesis 5:2 and Genesis 9:1.

The first two instances reveal that man was
created for the blessing. When God created Adam
and Eve, He blessed them. Then in Genesis 9:1,
God blessed Noah and his sons. This was about
2500 BC.

Genesis 12 is where it is recorded that God
made a covenant of blessing with Abraham. The
spoken blessing of God became a regular
occurrence from generation to generation.

In Genesis 12, God promised to bless Abraham
and to bless all of the families of the earth
through him. Paul records that when this
happened, God preached the Gospel to Abraham
(Galatians 3:8).

Scripture reveals that Abraham was blessed in
Genesis 14:17-20, Genesis 22:17-18 and Genesis
24:35. Then Isaac was blessed in Genesis 25:11
and 26:12-14. Jacob was blessed in Genesis
27:29 and Genesis 30:27. Joseph was blessed in
Genesis 39:2 and 5.

The blessing went from generation to
generation after God made a covenant of blessing
with Abraham.

all know that Jesus was blessed. In fact, if
[ ] udy the genealogy of Jesus in Matthew
chapter one, it traces the seed of Abraham. Jesus
is the seed of Abraham. When we study Galatians
chapter three, we find that Jesus was blessed as
the seed of Abraham, and we are blessed in Him.

Galatians 3:9

> *So then those who are of faith are
> blessed with faithful Abraham.*

Galatians 3:13-14

> *Christ has redeemed us from the curse
> of the Law, being made a curse for us:
> for it is written, Cursed is everyone who
> hangs on a tree: That the blessing of
> Abraham might come on the Gentiles
> through Jesus Christ, that we might
> receive the promise of the Spirit through
> faith.*

Galatians 3:16

> *Now to Abraham and his seed the
> promises were made. He did not say,
> And to seeds, as of many; but as of one,
> And to your Seed, which is Christ.*

Galatians 3:29

> *And if you are Christ's, then you are
> Abraham's seed, and heirs according to
> the promise.*

We are the seed of Abraham through faith in
Jesus Christ. In Jesus Christ we have inherited

Abraham's blessing. When we inherit something, we don't work to receive it. We just show up, believe it, and receive it.

So, before Abraham, in the first 2000 years of man's existence on the earth, it is only recorded three times that God blessed man. But then, when God made a covenant of blessing with Abraham, the covenant blessing went from generation to generation.

We inherit Abraham's blessing through faith in Jesus. When a person believes on Jesus they are blessed, spiritually speaking. If we renew our minds with that truth, we will begin to walk in the blessing of Abraham.

Abraham was a very rich man, and God made him that way (Genesis 13:2 and Genesis 24:35). If Abraham received a natural, physical, financial blessing through the covenant of God, so can we. We are the seed of Abraham, through faith in Jesus, and the promises of God in Christ are yes and amen to the glory of God by us.

God gets glory when we walk in His promises, and these promises include financial increase. You can see this clearly by simply reading the first fourteen verses of Deuteronomy 28!

Not only are we blessed in Christ, but we are also redeemed from the curse. The curse of the law, which is described after the blessing, in Deuteronomy 28 included sickness, poverty, slavery and death. Christ redeemed us from the curse of the law (Galatians 3:13).

Christ redeemed us from sickness, poverty, slavery to sin, and spiritual death. The last enemy of physical death will be put under His feet when He returns for His church.

If Jesus is our Lord, we are redeemed from the curse of the law. It is about time we start believing the promises and seeing the blessings of health and financial increase in life as well as forgiveness of sin and peace.

When we understand that blessing is included in the covenant, we realize that everyone can receive the blessing of the Lord. It is not some special promise for special people, but it is the promise of God for every believer. If you are a believer in Jesus, you have a covenant right to prosper.

The same blood that bought our forgiveness and our peace bought our healing and our prosperity. He was wounded for our transgressions and bruised for our iniquities. The chastisement of our peace was upon Him. By His stripes we are (were) healed. And He who was rich became poor so that we can be rich (Isaiah 53:4-5, 1 Peter 2:24, 2 Corinthians 8:9).

If Calvary didn't pay for it, then we don't have a right to it. But Calvary paid for our forgiveness, peace, healing, and prosperity. We need to believe all the promises of the Bible so we can receive what God wants us to receive and do what He wants us to do.

Sickness and poverty can limit our ability to share the Gospel and fulfill the Great Commission. We need to believe the promises so we can possess the promised land. We need to rise up and take authority and begin living like the sons and daughters of God that we are!

The Priestly Blessing

Genesis 14:18-20 (brackets added for clarity)

> And Melchizedek the king of Salem brought forth bread and wine. And he was the priest of the most high God. And he blessed him, and said, Blessed be Abram of the most high God, possessor of Heaven and earth. And blessed be the most high God, who has delivered your enemies into your hand. And he [Abram] gave him [Melchizedek] tithes of all.

Melchizedek was the king of Salem (Jerusalem, City of Peace). He was also priest of the Most High God. He spoke a blessing over Abram's life. The spoken blessing of Melchizedek was a confirmation of God's covenant of blessing on Abram's life.

We all need to remember where the blessing of the Lord comes from. It comes from Jesus. Because of Jesus, we have been brought into the covenant of blessing. In this covenant of blessing, we have been set free from the power of the enemy.

Abram had just won a major battle, delivering his nephew, Lot, from his enemies. When Abram heard of Lot's distress, he took three hundred eighteen trained men and recovered Lot, his property, his family, and the inhabitants of Sodom.

Not only did Abram get back what was stolen from Sodom, he got back more. Inevitably, those thieving kings had been robbing other cities too. When Melchizedek blessed him, he reminded him that God was the one who set him free. We not only need to remember where the blessing comes from, we need to remember where our freedom comes from.

After Melchizedek blessed Abram, Abram gave Melchizedek tithes of all. This was over four hundred years before tithing was required in the law of Moses. Notice the blessing came before the tithing. We need to remember this in our giving. We give *as a result of* the blessing, not to make the blessing happen!

Hebrews 7:4-10 reveals that the less is blessed by the greater. In other words, Melchizedek was greater than Abraham. It goes on to say that Levi paid tithes in Abraham. This is not actually talking about what Levi did. It is talking about what Abraham did. We could accurately say that Abraham's gift satisfied the debt of many generations.

You notice I said gift. Abraham did not give as a debt that he owed. He did not give out of a sense of obligation. He gave out of his heart. He gave because he was grateful, and because he wanted to. In fact, this is the only scripture that talks about paying tithes, and it is not talking about what Levi did. So, Abraham's gift satisfied Levi's debt.

Ultimately, Jesus' gift satisfied the debt of every generation. You may be a tither. But I want you to have a mind shift from the idea of "paying" tithes to "giving" tithes.

We give not as a debt, as something we owe God, but we give as a seed. The problem with debt thinking in relationship to our giving is that if we give with a debt mindset, we lose the blessing.

Giving as a seed has a harvest. When we give, we should give all of our seed with a harvest mentality. Giving as a seed has a future.

Numbers 6:22-27 (NKJV)

> *And the Lord spoke to Moses, saying: "Speak to Aaron and his sons, saying, 'This is the way you shall bless the children of Israel. Say to them: "The Lord bless you and keep you; The Lord make His face shine upon you, And be gracious to you; The Lord lift up His countenance upon you, And give you peace."' "So they shall put My name on the children of Israel, and I will bless them."*

The Old Testament priests were to proclaim a blessing over the children of Israel, God's covenant people. Today we are God's covenant people through faith in Jesus (Galatians 3:29). We are blessed in Christ. We are also a priesthood of believers with Jesus our Great High Priest. We are to bear the Word of God and proclaim the blessing of the Lord.

I want to break this blessing down in the Hebrew, so we get a better picture of what is happening here.

Bless comes from the Hebrew word *barak*, which means to kneel, bless, be blessed, cause to kneel, praise or salute. Picture someone bowing before the Lord in reverence and as they do the Lord pouring blessing on them. The New Testament equivalent is the blessing of grace that comes on those who humble themselves in the sight of the Lord.

As we surrender to Jesus, He makes His face to shine upon us. The Hebrew word for shine here is the word *owr*. It means to become light or bright, make to shine, to be glorious or to set on fire. We are set on fire with the glory of God as He looks on us in His grace.

Gracious comes from the word *chanan*. It means to be gracious, show favor, make favorable, direct favor to, or to have mercy on. Thank God, He has had mercy on us. He is making us favorable and directing favor our way. I often say, *"Life isn't fair, we have favor!"*

I have a saying that I teach on the favor of God. I have taught it around the world. I have seen people supernaturally blessed as then make this confession on a regular basis: *I have favor with God. I have favor with man, and I have a good understanding.*

We have seen students go from the bottom to the top of the class through this confession. We have seen businesses increase more and more as they speak these words of life and blessing. God is no respecter of persons, but He is a respecter of faith. So, keep speaking faith-filled words that agree with what God says about you.

The Hebrew word for peace here is the word *shalom*. It represents completeness, soundness, welfare, health, prosperity, peace, safety tranquility, and contentment. This is peace through a covenant relationship with God.

God revealed Himself to Gideon as *Jehovah Shalom*. Thank God, He is our peace and provision. We are well, healthy, prospering, and at peace through our relationship with Jesus. His covenant is bringing these things into reality in our lives.

The last Hebrew word that I want to focus on in Numbers 6 is the word "name." God says, "They will put My name on the children of Israel, and I will bless them." The Hebrew word is *shem*. It means reputation, fame, glory, memorial, or monument.

God says, "I'm putting My reputation on the line. This is how I treat My kids." God wants to use His children as an advertisement of how good that He is. He wants to make us memorials and monuments of His glory and goodness. We are to bring glory and honor to His name.

When we surrender to His love and life, we find favor in His face. He pours out His extravagant love and blessing on us.

Ultimately, Jesus is our Great High Priest, and we are priests to God (Hebrews 7:22-28, 1 Peter 2:5-10). We are called to show forth the praises of Him who called us out of darkness into His marvelous light.

As we minister to Him, we find favor in His face; then we share it with the world and bless in His name.

The Commanded Blessing

Every born-again believer has a right to the covenant of blessing. Since all believers are priests in the New Covenant, we speak this priestly blessing and we receive this blessing from Jesus, the Great High Priest of the New Covenant.

Now, let's look into the commanded blessing. The commanded blessing is part of the covenant of blessing.

Deuteronomy 28:8

> *The LORD shall command the blessing on you in your storehouses and in all that you set your hand to; and He shall bless you in the land which the LORD your God gives you.*

Jesus is the condition for these commanded blessings. In Deuteronomy 28:1-2, the scripture says if you shall listen diligently to the voice of the Lord your God, to observe and do all His commandments, the Lord your God will set you on high above all nations of the earth and all these blessings shall come you and overtake you, if you listen to the voice of the Lord your God.

Let's be honest with ourselves. Not one of us has ever listened to everything the Lord has told us and followed His voice perfectly. Not one person, other than Jesus, has ever kept all of the commandments. Not only have we fallen short through sins of commission, James 4:17 says that when we know to do good, and fail to do it, it is sin.

We have all fallen short. We have all missed the mark. We have all sinned.

If that is the case, then no one could qualify for these covenant blessings. However, we do not qualify by our performance, but we qualify through the performance of Jesus.

We believe in the vicarious suffering of Christ. In other words, when Jesus died on the cross, He took all of our sins. Not only did He take all of our sins, He gave us His righteousness as a gift. We are the righteousness of God in Christ Jesus (2 Corinthians 5:21). Jesus was the just dying for the unjust, being put to death in the flesh, but raised in the Spirit (1 Peter 3:18).

Believers receive the righteousness of God as a gift. Through His redemption we are redeemed from every curse and blessed with every blessing. Therefore, all of the promises of God are now ours. They are yes and amen in Christ Jesus to the glory of God by us (2 Corinthians 1:20).

God said, "Yes" to the promises in Christ. We say, "Amen" through our faith. When we believe on Jesus, and when we believe the promises are for us, we can move into everything God has promised. When we walk in these promises, it brings glory to God.

Remember, God wants to bless you so much that He makes you an advertisement of how He treats His kids.

The blood of Jesus qualifies us for the best blessings of God. Believers have left the dominion of darkness and been translated into the kingdom of the Son of His love. We have complete pardon for our sins, as if they were never committed, through the offering of His blood, according to the ultimate wealth of His grace (Colossians 1:12-14).

In this New Covenant, Jesus is the condition for the blessing. We are blessed and not cursed.

In Numbers 23, Balak, a foreign king, had hired Balaam, a foreign prophet, to come and curse the children of Israel. However, when Balaam came, he blessed the children of Israel three times. In verse 20, Balaam declared, "I have received a commandment to bless. He has blessed, and I cannot reverse it."

Israel was living under the commanded blessing of the Lord, so Balaam could not curse them. We are blessed and not cursed in Christ. Christ has redeemed us from the curse, so that the blessing of Abraham might come on the Gentiles (believers) through faith (Galatians 3:13-14).

Jesus took every curse so that we can receive every blessing, including those concerning financial prosperity. As a whole, the Jewish people live with this attitude: "I am a covenant person of God, and I am blessed by the Most High God."

As we begin to understand the New Covenant, especially what is written about it in Galatians 3, we should begin to live with this attitude: "I am a covenant person of God, and I am blessed by the Most High God."

That is what faith is. It is a major attitude. We have a major attitude of faith. We have a spirit of faith. My good friend, Mark Hankins, says that the spirit of faith will make you swing out over hell on a cornstalk and spit in the devil's eye!

The spirit of faith is a speaking spirit. Begin to speak God's Word. Begin speaking words of life and blessing. Begin to say about yourself what God says about you and move into the blessings of God (2 Corinthians 4:13).

Jubilee

Jesus is the fulfillment of the commanded blessing. In Leviticus 25:21, the scripture says, *"Then I will command My blessing on you in the sixth year, and it shall bring forth fruit for three years."* This sixth year is referring to the year of Jubilee.

Jesus is our Jubilee. In Numbers 25, there are seven results of Jubilee. These include:

1. Restored to the proper place in the family
2. Restored possessions
3. Eating the increase
4. Oppression will cease
5. Debts will be forgiven
6. Slaves go free
7. Supernatural increase

Since Jesus is our Jubilee, the believer has a right to all of these things, 100% of the time, not just once every fifty years. As believers, we can expect supernatural increase 100% of the time.

Do you remember my confession, "I have favor with God, I have favor with man, and I have a good understanding?"

I have a friend in our church who is over 80 years old. He said, "Pastor, I added this, and I say it every day: 'I have favor with God, I have favor with man, I have a good understanding, and I have supernatural increase.'"

This gentleman works five to six days a week. He is strong and healthy. He is a tremendous giver. His business is exploding, and he is experiencing supernatural increase. He is receiving what he speaks. Death and life are in the power of our tongue (Proverbs 18:21).

During the beginning of the Covid crisis, in March of 2020, I was preaching on the commanded blessing, the leaders of a popular teaching ministry were sitting on the front row. I looked at them and said, "You are going to have supernatural increase!" I could see it all over them.

They are traveling ministers, but travel was being shut down everywhere. Yet, in 2020, their ministry increased tremendously. They had more than a 65% increase from the previous year. Within two months of that word, their partnerships increased over 65%. It was truly supernatural.

I know that I have received supernatural increase. There is no way to explain the increase on my life, or on my children's lives, except that it is supernatural. It is the blessing of God. We live under the commanded blessing of the Lord. Since God is no respecter of persons, you can believe and receive supernatural increase as well.

In Psalm 133:3, the scripture declares, *"There the Lord commanded His blessing, even life forevermore."* This Psalm talks about brethren dwelling together in unity and the anointing running from the head down the skirts of Aaron. It says in this place there is a commanded blessing.

In December of 2019, when we were on the way to church, Barbara told me that I was to lay hands on another ministry couple for increase. In the year 2020, their ministry increased by seven times. That is supernatural increase!

We need to walk in unity with other like-minded believers. We need to get connected where the anointing of increase is flowing. My friend

Jesse Duplantis says, "The anointing of increase is on us."

I concur: The anointing of increase is on us. The anointing of increase is on Charis Christian Center. The anointing of increases is on Lawson and Barbara Perdue. And in Jesus Christ the anointing of increase is available to you.

We live under the commanded blessing through Jesus Christ. He meets the condition. He is the fulfillment. The anointing of increase flows from Him.

Chapter Nine

PURPOSE. VISION.
PLAN. VOLITION.

When I went to Dr. Lester Sumrall's Bible College, one of my instructors wrote these four words on a card: purpose, vision, plan, volition. Understanding this can help us move into financial increase.

Purpose

There is a purpose to prosperity.

Deuteronomy 8:18

> *But you shall remember the Lord your God: for it is He who gives you the power to get wealth, that He may establish His covenant which He swore to your fathers, as it is this day.*

God gives us the power to get wealth so that He can establish His covenant in the earth. If the church doesn't have adequate finances, it is going to be hard to complete the Great Commission. It takes money to preach the Gospel.

Translating the Gospel, plane tickets, writing books, and holding church services all take money. For too long, the church has not had enough to do what we need to do when we need to do it. The "if and but" problem has been a challenge. One person said, "If ifs and buts were candy and nuts, we would all have a Merry Christmas."

We moved to Colorado Springs twenty years ago with the purpose of planting a church. It was painfully slow in the beginning. I had almost no money and no people. But I did have faith.

I started handing out flyers to tell people what we were doing. I would hand out one hundred flyers per day, and I did that for one hundred days. We were in the Southwest part of town at that time. I put flyers on every house within a mile of the location where we were meeting.

After one hundred days of putting out the flyers, we had our first service. On our first Sunday morning, we had twenty people show up, including my family of five, and some who said, "We will not be back."

Our sound system was one speaker with a keyboard that I played myself. We had one mic. Barbara led the songs, and my boys played their instruments. We set the whole thing up every Sunday.

I remember one person coming and complaining about the worship. Some other churches probably had a $500,000 worship budget, and they would compare us to that. But we grew gradually, and we saved some money.

It took us one year of Bible studies and Sunday morning services before we reached forty people. I remember that Sunday so well. Mary Peterson gave me a word before service from Job 8:7, "Though your beginning was small, yet your latter end shall greatly increase." New Jerusalem Bible says, "Your former state shall be seen as nothing beside your new prosperity."

That Sunday was in February 2002. I remember that our nursery people were challenged. We probably had three kids on a blanket in a back room that was carpeted. But to me, it was victory. We set an attendance record!

Today we have about two thousand people who call the church home and about one thousand show up every week to worship. In addition to this, we are currently on five television venues, five days a week, and have at least seven live stream events each week. In recent years, we have been giving about $500,000 per year to missions and other ministries.

Ultimately, I know that it was God's plan for us to plant Charis Christian Center in Colorado Springs, and I believe that is the major reason why we have succeeded financially.

Proverbs 19:21 declares, "There are many plans in a man's mind, but the counsel of the Lord, it shall stand." If we don't get our purpose in agreement with the purpose of the Lord, I don't think we have true prosperity, no matter what we do. We need a clear-cut purpose that comes from God.

Vision

Proverbs 29:18

Where there is no vision, the people perish: but he that keeps the law, happy is he.

The Hebrew says something like this, "Where there is no prophetic insight and enlightenment, the people cast off all restraint, but he who keeps the law is happy."

Vision comes from the Word of God. I began to have a vision for provision when I first went to Bible Study at fourteen years old and heard the full Gospel preached. Not long after that, I was filled with the Holy Spirit.

The Word of God changed my life and created hope on the inside of me. It caused me to understand that there was a God who loved me and who cared enough about me to send Jesus to establish His covenant with me.

The promises of God came alive to me. Thank God, we don't have to be sick, poor, and defeated by the devil. There is a Bible full of promises, and

Jesus died and rose again for us to receive them. The Holy Spirit gives us the power to make them a reality in our lives.

As my relationship with Jesus and the Holy Spirit grows, the plans and purposes of God become more and more real to me. My vision to prosper personally and professionally has grown as I grow in my relationship with God. I believe that when a person is born again and filled with the Holy Spirit, the plan of God is full grown on the inside of them, but it takes a lifetime to walk it out.

Can you see your business or ministry doubling? Can you see it increasing by ten or even one hundred times the size it is today?

Bobby Jean Merck gave me a word in about 1992. She said, "Increase shall be a key word for you." And it has been! Bobbie Jean flows in the prophetic: prophetic insight and enlightenment. Seeing something in the spirit is a key to seeing it in the natural.

Faith sees the invisible, hears the inaudible, and does the impossible. Impossible things become possible when we put our trust in God. All things are possible to him who believes, and all things are possible with God (Mark 9:23; Mark 10:27).

My son, Peter, is a good example of vision. He graduated from Princeton University in 2013. The United States was just coming out of a long term downward spiral, financially. Peter was offered only two jobs: one working for a small financial firm in New York City, the other working for Burger King corporate in Miami.

Peter took the Burger King Corporate job. He said, "They are owned by Three G Capital, and they have a bunch of young people in leadership there. I will be promoted very quickly."

Peter prophesied his own destiny. He went to work as one of fifty new hires in 2013. In the past eight years, he went from there to work for another of the Restaurant Brands International (a subsidiary of Three G Capital) companies, Tim Hortons Coffee in Toronto, Canada.

Two years later, they sent him to Southern California to oversee two hundred ninety Burger King locations. In about a year, they put him over eleven states and two thousand locations. Then Corporate moved him to Singapore to oversee eleven countries of Burger King Asia.

Peter was promoted twice during the Covid 19 pandemic and placed over sixteen countries of Burger King Asia. Most recently, they named him Vice President of Finance of Burger King of the Americas. He is receiving what He saw and what he said.

Not only do we need vision professionally, but we need vision personally. Can you see your debts paid? Can you see your car paid off? Can you see your house paid off? Can you see yourself giving $10,000, or $50,000, $250,000, or even a million dollars? Can you see yourself paying off someone's car, house or ministry?

We have had the privilege of sowing in unique ways. When we started our building program on Elkton Drive in Colorado Springs, I doubled my personal giving to $200 per week. I remember when I put that check in, the Holy Spirit spoke to me and I heard him say, "Soon, you will be giving what you make now."

When I started in the ministry, I was making $800 per month. In the end of 2008, I began giving $200 per week personally. My personal income with cattle, investments and ministry was about $50,000 per year.

In 2017, when we bought the Federal Drive property for our church in Colorado Springs, I remember God speaking to me to personally begin giving $1000 per week . For the last several years, Barbara and I have personally given over $50,000 per year. That is over four times what we made in salary when we started in the ministry.

I believe if I stay on track with God, my personal giving will far exceed where I am today.

Now, I did not tell you any of this to boast. We just need to get a vision for giving. If we can see it, we might just do it!

Not only does God give seed to sowers, He increases the seed sown and gives bread to the eaters. If you become a sower, you will not have to worry about what you are going to eat. I have never seen the righteous forsaken, or His seed begging bread (2 Corinthians 9:6-10, Psalm 37:25).

Plan

We need vision, but we also need a plan. A vision without a plan is just a pipe dream. One reason Joseph had so much success in the Egyptian Empire is because he had a plan.

We need a plan for our church, ministry or business. One banker friend loans a lot of money to people who have a certain financial planner who works with them in business. He does so because he recognizes that people who work with this planner have over a 90% success rate.

When we moved to Colorado Springs to start Charis Christian Center, I had to go to six banks before I found someone who would loan me the money to buy a home, and I had had a 50% down payment. Over 90% of church plants in Colorado Springs at that time failed. But God has the plan for our business, ministry, church, and personal lives, but we need to seek it.

Proverbs 16:9

> *A man's heart devises his way, but the* LORD *directs his steps.*

After Charis Christian Center had been going for a year and a half, I had $25,000 saved toward a building. I remember one person came and told me he wanted to see our vision statement. I told him to stay around, and he would see it.

After two-and-a-half years, we had $75,000 saved for a building. After three-and-a-half years, we had $150,000 saved, and after seven years, we had nearly a million dollars saved toward a building fund.

I can almost hear some people saying, "Well, brother, church is not a building." I fully agree! Church is the body of Christ. A church also is a community of faith. However, if you are going to make a major difference in a major city in the US or in the world, it is going to take some resources to do it.

While we were saving for a building, we were using our own home for midweek services. We also had offices and counseled people from our home for over 3 years. So, whereas this is proof that these things can be done from a private residence, it is sometimes less than ideal for keeping a good healthy family-ministry balance.

For example, once when I was counseling a couple for marriage in our living room, the man screamed at his wife while our children were in the basement. In an ideal situation, these situations are not those to which you want to expose your children.

Andrew Wommack told me when I moved to Colorado Springs that I would need to teach more on the subject of finances. He gave me two very good reasons: first, people need to be taught about this so that they can personally prosper. Secondly, if we were going to make a difference in a city like Colorado Springs, it would take some money!

God has been so faithful to us. As I write this book, I am sitting in my office in Charis Christian Center. Our building is over 120,000 square feet. Although we purchased it at a miraculous discount, it would likely cost over $60 million dollars to build this building today!

The good news is our building is debt free. We also have two other ministries that have offices in our building. One is an evangelistic teaching ministry and the other is a prophetic ministry. We need the fivefold ministry to work together to build the body of Christ.

And we aren't finished, yet. We also have money saved toward the next big opportunity that God will give Charis Christian Center to reach Colorado Springs and the world with the message of Jesus.

We have a plan.

We save at least 20% of the income that comes into the church. We invest it in different things. We seek to hear God's voice, so that we can follow His instructions and reap the end-time harvest.

These are other areas our plan includes: giving between 10-20%; personnel costs 25%; general church needs 20%; and outreach 20%.

To keep it simple, I think two things are necessary in a church finance plan: give at least 10%, and keep your personnel costs to under 35%. The rest should work out in the middle.

Those are the two greatest mistakes I see made in church finance. We either don't give enough, or we spend too much on personnel. You must plant seed (giving) to reap a harvest. And if you spend too much on personnel, there is not enough money to do outreach (win souls).

Now, there may be some cases in smaller communities where a church needs to spend more than 35% on personnel, but that is the exception, not the rule.

Not only do we need a plan to prosper as a church, but we need a plan to prosper personally. My personal plan is to give at least 10%, invest at least 10%, and live off 80% or less. If you do this for a long time, you will prosper.

Now, you *can* give more than 10%. Barbara and I give much more than 10% personally, but the increase in giving needs to come out of the 80%. Also, make sure you save something. This might look like something as simple as paying additional principle on your house payments.

Experts have told me that the single thing the average American family can do to gain wealth is to own their home. Think about it this way: if you are renting long term, you are buying the property for someone else.

In conclusion, you must develop a plan. Give to God first, at least 10%. Save or invest at least 10%. Spend less than you make and do it for a long time. The end results might amaze you.

Volition

Our will has a lot to do with what we receive from God. Someone called the other day and asked me why their friend—who I have no personal relationship with—is not receiving healing. I told the person, "I don't know."

I'm not God, and I don't know everything. However, I do know a few things. I know that it is God's will for everyone to be saved and to come to a knowledge of the truth (1 Timothy 2:4). I know that Jesus provided for our physical healing at the same time He provided forgiveness of sin (Isaiah 53:4-5, 1 Peter 2:24). I know that God wants us to live a good, long, healthy life and to prosper (Psalm 90:10, Psalm 91:16, 3 John 2).

However, for us to receive these things, we need to get our will in agreement with the will of God.

God has a plan, and it is good. We have a will to believe what God promised and to walk in His plan. It is a decision we make to believe God. When we do that long term, I believe we will have good results. If you are willing and obedient, you will eat of the good of the land (Isaiah 1:19).

Years ago, I stopped at a gas station and there was a young man, probably sixteen or seventeen years old, at the cash register. I told him if he would start with a hundred dollars and invest $68 per month in an investment with a 10% return, he would have a million dollars in fifty years. He said he wasn't interested in saving money because he wanted to buy tennis shoes. This young man had time on his side, but he didn't have the will.

I bet someone is thinking, *10% is a large return!* I try to make 10% on average. I have some things that make 6%, and some things that make 17%, but over the years, I have been consistently able to average a 10% return on my investments. **If you don't think you can, you probably won't.**

I also tell people that it is easy to make a million dollars. How is that? Just figure out how to make a thousand dollars and do it a thousand times. You may think I'm crazy, but it has worked for me!

Disciplined action over a long period of time produces amazing results. There are very simple, seemingly insignificant, actions you can take which will help you save money over time. For example, Barbara and I nearly always drink water when eating out. In our earlier years, we usually shared a meal to cut down on costs as well.

Several years ago, a couple came into my office for financial counseling. They were drinking $5 coffees and complaining about how other people had held them back. I told them that the other people didn't buy the coffees in their hands!

If you are really in a crunch and trying to eliminate debt, you might want to just eat at home. My son Aaron believed God to pay off the balance of his college debt. With supernatural intervention, he did it in six months. It was certainly God, but during those six months he was also very disciplined with his spending. He only ate out twice, both at six-dollar burrito place!

One leading financial teacher says if you are trying to eliminate major financial debt, you shouldn't even see the inside of a restaurant unless you work there.

Summary

First, find your God-given purpose. What do you like to do? What are you good at? What do other people see in you that is a unique or special talent? What doors are open to you? These are keys to finding purpose.

Second, get a vision. Begin to see from the realm of the spirit, both personally and professionally. Can you see your personal net worth being one hundred thousand dollars? A million dollars? Ten million dollars? Thirty million dollars? One hundred million dollars or more?

Don't be afraid to dream big!

I watched a film which criticized preachers who are prosperous, and the richest preacher they examined had a personal net worth of $800 million. Yet, this kind of prosperity occurs in the secular world all the time, and no one bats an eye.

My son, Andrew, works for a man who has a personal net worth of over $800 million dollars, and his own personal jet, but nobody even thinks anything about it because it is in the business world. My son, Peter, works for a man whose net worth is more than $25 billion, and nobody thinks anything about that, either. But God forbid that a preacher would have anything!

Many times, the problem with the church in the realm of finance is that we think too little. My personal assistant recently attended a business meeting where the business is bringing in $58 million per year, and they are expecting to increase to $85 million per year in the next three years.

The business world doesn't have a problem thinking big in the money realm, but the church has been deceived!

We equate poverty to holiness and wonder why we can't get out of debt! Believers often have a debt mentality that is very detrimental to advancing the Kingdom of God.

For example, I once tried to help a ministry pay off their building. The board of directors responded with this message, "We think that the debt is a good use of our resources." So, I went and found another ministry and helped them pay off their building instead!

Wouldn't it be nice to kill that interest that is working against you and get some investments working for you? Get a vision to prosper!

Third, make a plan. It will need some revision as you go along, but at least *think* about breaking out in the realm of financial increase. How could you make a million, or ten million, or a hundred million dollars? How could you grow your net worth to ten times what it is today?

Finally, volition. This process takes will-power and discipline. It takes work. Faith without corresponding action isn't faith at all—it's dead (James 2:17). Believe God and take steps toward your future.

Start somewhere. Start with something. Figure out what works for you and stay at it!

Chapter

Ten

PRACTICAL ASPECTS OF PROSPERITY

S omeone once said that some people are so earthly minded that they are no spiritual good. I heard Dr. Lester Sumrall say, "Some people are so spiritually minded that they are no earthly good!" There are two sides to every coin. In every area of life, we need balance.

Along with spiritual direction, we also need practical application. I am a very practical person. Especially in the realm of finance, we need some practical tools if we are to be successful.

The Rule of 72

This is the rule that shows how long it takes something to double. If you make 8% interest on an investment and compound it, it will take nine years for it to double. If you make 6% interest on an investment and compound it, it will take twelve years to double it.

This principle both works for you, and it works against you. If you are paying 24% interest on a credit card, it only takes three years for that debt to double! So, a very good practical rule in finance is to never pay interest on consumer debt. Figure out how to live within your means and do it. God will make a way for you to pay cash without relying on credit if you will believe Him!

Remember, I like to make 10% interest on my average investments. If I do that consistently, considering the rule of 72, once I begin saving money, I can double my investments every 7.2 years.

I have some real estate investments that consistently bring in 5-6% of their value over time. However, that value is before calculating appreciation. So, even though they may not be home run returns, when you add in the appreciation, they have made 8-15% total annual returns over time.

Appreciation

I'm sure you have heard the saying, "What goes up must come down." When it comes to gravity, that is absolutely true. However, in finances, over time, average good investments tend to go up more than they go down. Long term things go up.

Let me give you some examples. I had a neighbor who built a house in 1972 for $35,000. That same house sold in 2016 for $450,000 dollars. It brought over ten times what it initially cost to build.

That same neighbor gave me some good real estate investment advice. He said that he never tried to figure out how to totally pay for the real estate he purchased; he just wanted to know how to cover the expenses, interest and taxes and have some extra profit.

It really worked for him. He bought a Colorado Ranch in the 1960's for $34,900. He did a 1031 exchange on the property in the early 1980's and traded it for a Nebraska ranch that was worth one million dollars at the time. In 2007, he began working on a deal to do a 1031 exchange on the Nebraska ranch for a three-million-dollar Kansas ranch.

Ultimately, he took a $34,900 investment and made it worth 3 million dollars, and he did it all tax free! He and his family reaped the benefits. He had good thinking in the area of finances. He had a plan, and he worked it.

Another place that appreciation can be realized is the stock market.

In the beginning of 1980, the Dow Jones Industrial Average was just under 825. I remember that my mom went to a meeting where people were encouraging her to invest. However, there were preachers calling investing in the stock market "Babylon" and saying that it was going to fall. These ministers advised against investing because of what they saw as a huge risk.

Granted, there have been many ups and downs in the stock market over the years. But there have been a lot more ups than downs. For example, as I am writing in 2021, this week the Dow Jones closed over 35,000. That means that if you would have invested $825 in 1980 that it would be worth over $35,000 today, less expenses.

I have watched the church take a back seat and complain about the evil in the world. I have seen them many times be so conservative that they are literally foolish. People in the church will be take a 1% return while people in the world are getting returns over 10%. That is just crazy!

I understand that with risk comes reward. I have taken risks, both personally and professionally. But most people in their later years don't wish they had played it safer. Most regret that they played it too safe!

In his 80's, my grandfather regretted that he didn't buy all the land around him in the 1930's. He could have purchased several thousand acres for $1 per acre. At the time, he was unique in that he had the money in the bank to do it.

However, he didn't do it because he said that his parents taught him that if you just take care of what you have, you will always have enough, but warned against taking too much risk. He always had enough, but he was limited by limited thinking.

Learning from my grandfather, I made a decision in my late teens that I was going to take risks in my life. I didn't want to find myself at the age of eighty saying, "I wish I would have done that."

A couple of times, I have suffered some major losses and thought, *I maybe shouldn't have done that.* However, being an overall higher-than-average risk taker has served me well.

We need to understand the value of appreciation and take advantage of it. My personal thinking in the realm of debt is to try not to take debt on things that depreciate in value. Occasionally, that may not be an option, but most of the time it is.

Have a Good Tax Plan

One of my financial mentors told me that he didn't believe anyone in America could really get ahead without having a good tax plan.

When I was about seventeen years old, I did my own taxes and sent the IRS a couple thousand dollars. I knew other people making a lot more money than I was who didn't pay that much. They used good accountants!

The next year, I hired one of the best CPA's in our county. I stayed with him for thirty years. In my late 40's, I wanted to make a major change in direction financially, but if I had immediately quit my business, most of those business assets would have been spent on taxes. I talked to my CPA, and one of my investment advisors. They developed a plan and helped me move the money to retirement accounts over about ten years. I still paid some tax, and when I take the money out of the retirements I will pay some taxes, but I kept the majority of the money working for me.

Good professional people will cost you a little money up front, but they will save and make you much more than they cost.

Over time, your strategies will need to adjust to work with the systems and laws in place at the time. However, wealthy people find a way to keep their wealth working for them.

Multiple Streams of Income

There are three basic streams of income: work, business, and investment. Work is where we should get the money to cover our basic expenses. Business is where we can realize increase. Investment is where we develop passive income.

One of my good friends told me that if you find work you enjoy, it won't be hard for you to prosper. When we enjoy our work, it makes the days seem shorter. There will be aspects of any work that will be more challenging. However, when we are doing something that we like to do, or feel called to do, it will make our work much more rewarding.

I enjoy pastoring, and I feel called to do it. Most weeks I work six days a week. I have never complained about it because I enjoy the work. Over time, my income has grown, and though only a modest portion of my income comes from ministry, I love it. I have been able to minister to others and to live from it. What a blessing!

Business is where one can develop increase. This increase can help us in dream building over time.

Ecclesiastes 5:3

> For a dream comes through the multitude of business...

Before I went into full time ministry, I worked farming and ranching. When I was fourteen years old, I started in the cattle business.

To start, I bought three calves. One of them ran away, one of them died, and one of them lived and made money. But I didn't quit.

Later, I bought ten cows, and then worked up to thirty cows before I went to Bible School.

When we moved from Colorado to South Bend, Indiana, where I went to Bible School and worked for Dr. Lester Sumrall, I sold those cows and paid off the double wide trailer that Barbara and I lived in. We rented that double wide while we were in Bible School and sold it for $30,000 when we started Church of the Redeemed in Kit Carson.

After the sale, we gave $5000 to the church in Kit Carson. (We were making $800-$1000 per month at the time.) Then we split the remaining $25,000 dollars. We put about half of it in the house we bought in Kit Carson and half of it in the cattle business.

Today, that $25,000 has increased to over $2,000,000! Currently, about half is in real estate and about half is now in investments.

Investment income is the third stream of income, which is passive income. In other words, someone else does the work, and you receive the profit.

When my son, Andrew, graduated from High School, one of the families in the church gave him a book on the topic of financial stewardship.

He read the book in two days, and said, "Dad, you do everything in this book."

I asked him what it said. He told me the ten principles written in the book, and I said, "Yes, I do. There are basic principles of financial increase in the Bible. If you live by them, you will prosper!"

In Deuteronomy 28:8, God says that He will command the blessing on our storehouses, and on all that we set our hands to do (our work). There are different types of storehouses, and everyone needs them.

Savings accounts can be a basic storehouse. They can be used to save money for a down payment on a house, or to build money to put in a business or other investments. Storehouses can also be real estate investments or retirement accounts.

One storehouse could be your personal home. Remember, over time, real estate generally appreciates. A stick-built home will usually appreciate over time. If you make extra principal payments, it can be a great investment strategy.

There are a lot of different areas where you can have investment income. Some of the best ones in the United States are in the forms of retirement plans. Some of these can be realized through employment opportunities, such as a 401(k).

I have never had an employer-sponsored 401(k). However, my CPA and my investment advisor had me start a personal 401(k). There are different types of these accounts that are advantageous.

One type of 401(k) is called a ROTH 401(k). If a person is on the lower aspect of income, they can do a ROTH IRA. I had all three of my sons start ROTH IRAs when they were in High School. The advantage of the ROTH program is that you pay the tax up front, but you do not pay tax on the increase. That can be a huge benefit during the later years of life when that retirement is withdrawn.

If you have a plan, over time you should be able to develop these three areas of income. Work income is what we eat from. Business income is where we increase. Investment income is where we develop passive income.

Remember, one thing I do from all three streams of income is give into the Kingdom.

Diversity of Investments

Ecclesiastes 11:1-2

Cast your bread upon the waters: for you shall find it after many days. Give a portion to seven, and also to eight; for you know not what evil shall be upon the earth.

When we cast our bread upon the waters, we are giving to life-giving ministries that are taking the Gospel to the world. When we give into these ministries of life, it will come back to us in many days, in many ways.

When we invest, we need to spread our investments around. I have managed several million dollars of other people's money as well as some of my own. One personal rule I have is that no matter how right I think I am, or how much I think I have heard God, I never invest over 20% of my net worth into a single investment. We need to be diversely invested. This is wise because it allows protection from risking all in one place.

Another thing I personally do is to use several investment professionals from several different companies. I seek to glean wisdom from these people and "hear" God through them. I also give several different professionals money to invest for me and use different strategies from different ones. This is another form of diversification.

In major downturns in the stock market, the professionals usually only lose half as much as individual investors. Using professional people with wisdom from different areas with different strategies, and never putting over 20% in one investment, has worked as a good hedge of protection for me.

Chapter
Eleven

LIVING TO GIVE

I have found that when giving is the goal, living is no problem. There are three aspects of giving: Giving to give, giving to live, and living to give.

Ephesians 4:28

> *Let him who stole steal no more: but rather let him labor, working with his hands the thing which is good, that he may have to give to him who needs.*

The reason we work is so that we can give. Some people are working to make a living, but that is a terrible mentality. The problem is that the central focus is selfish. When we live to give, the central focus is generosity.

The fact of the matter is that generous people are blessed people. Those who are generous givers always seem to have enough. This is a biblical principle that works for both believers and unbelievers alike!

Proverbs 11:24-25

There is he who scatters and yet increases; and there is he who withholds more than is sufficient, but it tends to poverty. The liberal soul shall be made fat: and he who waters others shall be watered also himself.

Several years ago, there was a study done on Fortune 500 companies. One common denominator was that almost all these companies practiced the principle of giving.

While over 90% of these companies practiced giving on a regular basis, about 80% of church people do not practice tithing—giving 10% of their income to God. No wonder the world often has more financial increase than the church! It is because they operate by biblical principles, even without realizing it.

As I mentioned previously, I learned at a young age to be a giver, and it has served me well. When we begin to understand the principles in 2 Corinthians chapters 8-9 on sowing and reaping, we can move into the principle of living to give.

Giving to Give

When my wife Barbara was a young teenager, she went to church with a friend. Her friend put a dollar in the offering and then waved goodbye to it as the plate went down the row. Barbara realized that her friend was just giving to give.

This girl thought when she gave, her money was lost and would never been seen or heard from again. She waved farewell because she did not understand the principle of sowing.

Many people in the church today give because they feel it is something they owe God. They are simply "giving to give." They don't understand the principle of sowing and reaping, so they fail to receive a harvest. However, if we understand the principle of sowing, we can sow to reap a harvest.

Giving to Live

In the early 1980's, I attended a full Gospel church that had a strong emphasis on faith. My pastor was the overseer of ten churches in the area. One of the pastors was struggling with finances. My pastor asked him if he tithed. When he replied in the affirmative, my pastor asked him about the attitude with which he was giving.

The other pastor replied that he had been taught that the tithe was a debt that he owed to God. He said that the sowing principle didn't come into place until after you gave the first 10%. He was simply giving to give.

My pastor told him to change his attitude and to begin to give everything as a seed.

The next month, my pastor asked how the other's pastor's finances were. He replied that they were fine. He had changed nothing but the attitude with which he gave, and he immediately began to receive increase on his seed! Giving with this kind of attitude is what we call giving to live.

Living to Give

The greatest attitude in giving is living to give. When we move through stages one and two, we can get into this area, stage three. I believe this is the highest area of giving.

In 2010, Charis Christian Center moved into the property at 720 Elkton Drive. We bought two buildings, totaling 17,500 square feet, did a buildout tying them together and ended up with over 27,000 square feet. The total project cost about $2.35 million.

When we moved into the church, we owed just over $600,000. God spoke to me to pay it off and to save at least 20% of our income. (Remember the Joseph principle.)

One Sunday in 2012, I told the congregation that we had only one payment left to make. God spoke to someone in the church to make that payment. Later he realized he didn't even ask how much it was! However, he called me on Monday, and we went to the bank together. The last payment was about $3,300. I tried to talk him out of paying it all the way to the bank. However, he was determined to sow that seed.

He made the payment. On the way back to the church from the bank, about a fifteen to twenty-minute drive, I gave him a word that God was going to give him his family a home that would be worth $330,000 dollars. Within three years—through a series of supernatural events—they had a debt-free home worth $330,000!

God is not mocked; we sow what we reap. One friend of mine years ago said, "You can't beat God at giving."

When you get your heart right and learn these principles, supernatural increase will abound to you. One person defined prosperity as one hand to give, one hand to receive, and enough for you when it flows through.

I have been around some generous people, and they are all incredibly blessed. Generous people are blessed people. They do not live in the land of not enough or barely enough; they live in the land of more than enough. Our God is more than enough!

Chapter
Twelve

DEALING WITH
DIFFICULTY

When I was in my early teens, I read a book by a spirit-filled author who talked about an investor who always prayed before he invested and never made a losing investment. I thought, *I want to be that person!*

Now, I have lived a few years, and have taken more risks than most people, and God has been good to me. But to be honest with you, I don't think that person ever existed. Even the best investors lose money once in a while!

There are a couple challenges with this kind of thinking that we can make winning decisions 100% of the time.

First of all, we are spirit, soul and body. We are not 100% spirit. So, we do miss God once in a while because we not only hear from our spirits, but from our souls and bodies as well.

Second, if you think like that, and something goes wrong, the tendency is to give up totally or get condemned and quit moving toward the goal. The truth is mistakes can (and will) be made. The important thing is to be able to believe God to turn things around in your favor!

In the year 1997, we had a major blizzard in Eastern Colorado. I was pastoring in Kit Carson but also owned cattle. I lost about $100,000 immediately. In the winter of 2004-2005, there was yet another blizzard. At that time, we were living in Colorado Springs, and I was invested in cattle in a bigger way. I had over 3000 head, and a lot of debt to go with it. I lost about $250,000.

In the 1997 blizzard I had a preacher friend from the neighboring town. He told me he thought God was trying to speak to me to get out of the cattle business. Today I am very lightly invested in agriculture. However, if you think that just because it is difficult God is telling you to quit, you are mistaken!

God has certainly been gracious to me. He has prospered me and protected me. However, there has certainly been some difficulty along the way.

When we had the blizzard in 1997, it took me about a year to recover all my losses. The blizzard from 2004-2005 took me several years to recover my losses. I did however recover all my losses and made some extra back.

One year, while living in Kit Carson, I was praying about buying cattle in February to put on pasture that summer. Early one morning, God woke me up and told me to read my Bible for that day. I was reading in Isaiah 30. Verse 23 really spoke to me. It said, "Your cattle shall feed in large pastures."

I took that as a word from God and bought all the cattle that I could with my equity. I had about $40,000 to begin and borrowed $100,000. After I bought the cattle, it just stayed dry. The dirt was blowing, cattle kept getting cheaper, and corn was getting more expensive. By the first part of April, I had lost all my equity, and my banker was not too happy.

I went to another bank and talked to that banker. I said, "Cattle are cheap, and corn is high, but I believe it's going to rain!" He loaned me the money, and I changed banks. Then on May 28, it started raining. It rained all summer. The desert blossomed like a rose.

By the next spring when I sold those cattle, I had *doubled* my equity.

God gave me a word: "If you make it through the famine, you will make it to the feast." And it came to pass.

There are a couple words in the Bible about famine that one should take to heart.

Psalm 33:19

> *To deliver their soul from death, and to keep them alive in famine.*

Psalm 37:19

They shall not be ashamed in the evil time: and in the days of famine they shall be satisfied.

Job 5:22

At destruction and famine you shall laugh...

Keys to Dealing with Difficulty

The first key is to learn how to stay alive in the famine. Don't give up. Keep believing God, and do not quit. Find a way to hold on if at all possible.

The second key is to be satisfied in famine. In Philippians 4:12-13, Paul said, *"I know both how to be abased, I know how to abound...I can do all things through Christ who strengthens me."* If you don't learn how to be abased, you really don't know how to abound.

The third key is to laugh at the famine! Joseph laughed at the famine because he was ready. He had news from God beforehand. In fact, the famine made Pharaoh the richest man on the planet, and Joseph was his go-to guy. The children of Israel ended up living in Goshen, the best of the land.

When we have a relationship with God, and we know how to believe Him, God can take what the enemy might have meant to destroy us and use it to bless us.

During that dark time when I lost all of my equity in the cattle business, God gave me a word from Psalm 112:4: *"Unto the upright there arises a light in the darkness: he is gracious, and full of compassion, and righteous."* I just saw it so clearly; it was like I was going through a tunnel, but there was light at the end of the tunnel, and God was going to bring me through. And He did.

In the beginning of 2020, I had about $1.4 million invested in the stock market for a business investment. Due to the pandemic, these investments went down to about $1 million at the end of March. Many people began to sell.

Then I received a word from God, "Don't bailout on the bottom." By the end of the year the investment recovered all and had increased to over $1.6 million.

John 16:33

> *...In the world you shall have tribulation: but be of good cheer; I have overcome the world.*

Don't Quit

Everything has ups and downs, and there will certainly be challenges in this world. But one thing has helped me succeed over the years, and it's that I did not quit.

When I went to Dr. Lester Sumrall's Bible College, I worked in the audio and video department. He had a message that I listened to over and over again. I think it's the best I have ever heard Dr. Sumrall preach. The sermon was called *I Did Not Quit.*

Dr. Sumrall talked about all of the times in over fifty years of ministry that he had problems. Either people spoke badly about him, or just bad things happened. But his undeniable faith would not stop. He did not quit.

Dr. Sumrall talked about when he first started out preaching, he might have been considered one of the least likely to succeed. He shared how people who he thought knew more than him said mean things, but God would encourage him.

He talked about how over the years, the people who had started out with him were mostly in the nursing home or the grave, but he just kept going, running with the vision of God. At the time he preached this, in my opinion, he was one of the most successful ministers in the world.

Dr. Sumrall never quit, and he stayed diligent in his calling. There is a great lesson in diligence. Proverbs says quite a few things about the power of diligence:

Proverbs 10:4

> *...The hand of the diligent makes rich.*

Proverbs 12:24

> *The hand of the diligent shall bear rule...*

Proverbs 12:27

...The substance of a diligent man is precious.

Proverbs 13:4

...The soul of the diligent shall be made fat.

Proverbs 21:5

The thoughts of the diligent tend only to plenty...

Proverbs 22:29

See a man diligent in his business? he shall stand before kings...

Proverbs 27:23-24

Be diligent to know the state of your flocks, and look well to your herds. For riches are not forever: and does the crown endure to every generation?

Be diligent and stay the course. God has good things in store for those who finish the race.

Chapter
Thirteen

MENTORS

The stronger the people are who you surround yourself with the stronger you become. We need people around us to help us get where God wants us to go.

Proverbs 13:20

> *He who walks with wise men shall be wise: but a companion of fools shall be destroyed.*

Years ago, I listened to a lesson by Dr. James Dobson. He said, "Everyone needs a Paul, everyone needs a Silas, and everyone needs a Timothy."

Everyone needs a Paul. We need older people in our lives who have walked the way before us, to help us along the way.

Everyone needs a Silas. We need friends who are going the same direction to help us find direction and keep us on the right path. These may be friends who keep us accountable.

Everyone needs a Timothy. We need younger people who we are sowing into. We need people who we are investing in to help them walk in the victory God has provided for them in Christ.

God has blessed me over the years with great mentors. He has given me financial mentors, and He has given me mentors in the ministry.

I believe that God gives everyone the opportunity to have good relationships who help us get to where He wants us to go. However, we need to be ready to receive these people who God places in our lives.

I have known some people who have had opportunity to have good mentors in their lives, but they are not open to sharing. Sometimes, they just don't want to change. Sometimes, they are just ignorant. But I have seen some of these people fail miserably because they were not willing to accept wise counsel; they were not seeking to hear the voice of God through divine connections.

Pauls

I have had two mentors in the ministry who I have watched and gleaned from. The first was Dr. Lester Sumrall. I saw in Dr. Sumrall a passion for the lost. I saw the heart of a true evangelist. I learned from him the power of purpose.

My other ministry mentor is Andrew Wommack. I was spirit-filled and called to preach in his ministry when I was only fourteen years old. Andrew has been a tremendous example to follow. He has also encouraged me along the way. I appreciate things I have learned from him by observation, and by his personal encouragement. The greatest thing that I have observed in Andrew is his passion for the truth of God's Word.

I also have had several others help me in the realm of finances. My father died when I was only seventeen years old, but God has provided some great men to help me along the way.

When I moved to Kit Carson, Colorado to plant Church of the Redeemed, I also started in the cattle feeding business. I learned from three men: Jim and Ervin Mitchek, and Aubrey Shotton. These men did things a little differently, but each man was successful in agriculture and with cattle, and I learned something from all of them.

If you want to be successful in a business, find three people who have succeeded in it. Find out how they succeeded and see what you can use from their experience that will help you succeed.

When I moved to Colorado Springs, God gave me two men who have helped me immensely. I was attending a birthday party for a wonderful man named Herb Carter a few years after we moved to Colorado Springs. We discovered that Herb was born on the same day as my dad, January 18, 1941.

Herb has helped me in a number of areas. He and his wife Judith have served tirelessly and faithfully directing the prayer team at our church, and they have been a tremendous blessing.

Ed Meyer is the other person who has helped me tremendously in Colorado Springs. Ed has served on our board and has always given me sound advice. He ran a very successful company before retiring. When he retired from his regular job, he helped our church with the buildout on the Federal Drive building. Ed and his wife Peggy have been a constant source of encouragement and wise counsel.

I truly appreciate the people God has brought into my life. It is important that you allow the Lord to bring these people into your life as well. Seek wise counsel!

Silases

Not only do we need older people who have walked the way before us, to encourage us and show us the way, we also need friends who help keep us on the right track.

Greg Fritz has been one such friend to me. He has served our ministry for over twenty years and has given very sound advice. I also have been able to help him in a few critical moments in his life and ministry.

Dr. Doug Weiss and his wife Lisa have also been tremendous friends. Doug has often given me sound advice along the way. Sometimes helping me see something from a different perspective, or just being there for me. I appreciate his friendship.

Timothys

Finally, we all need people who we are sowing into and helping to walk in the victory Jesus has provided. Not only am I deeply invested in my three sons, I have also helped a number of young pastors and ministers move successfully into that which God has called them.

In fact, my basic definition for success is this: The more successful you make other people, the more successful you become. As a successful husband, I make my wife successful. As a successful father, I make my children successful. As a successful pastor, I make my parishioners successful, and as a successful Bible School teacher, I help make my students successful.

One thing to remember in this whole scenario is this: you can share the truth with others, but you cannot make choices for them. Ultimately, it is their choice. Their choices will either make or break them!

Chapter

Fourteen

BLESSINGS AND
MIRACLES

I n 2 Kings 4, a widow woman came to the prophet Elisha with a problem. Her husband was a prophet who had died and left her and her children in debt. The creditors had come to take her sons to be slaves in payment.

What Do You Want?

Elisha asked her a question, "What shall I do for you?" Jesus asked that same question a number of times in the Gospels: "What do you want?"

If we want to receive from God, we need a clear picture of what we want.

Elisha then asked another question, "What do you have in your house?" God is not looking for what we do *not* have. He works with what we *do* have.

She replied, "I have nothing but a pot of oil." So, the prophet instructed the widow to go near and far to borrow empty containers from all of her neighbors. He said, "Borrow not a few." In other words, "Get a bunch of them!"

Once she gathered the containers, she went into her house, shut the door, and poured from her little pot of oil into the empty ones. As a result, there was a miracle in her house. When she obeyed the word of the prophet, every empty container was filled.

Elisha then instructed her to sell the oil, pay the debt, and live off the rest. Not only did she pay the debt, she received a retirement that not only took care of her, but also her sons. Her vision determined the bounds of her blessing. She received a miracle of supernatural increase.

Miracles of Increase

Jesus operated in miracles of increase. He not only forgave sinners and healed the sick, He fed the hungry as well. In John 6, Jesus had been ministering all day to the multitudes. There were over 5000 people gathered and receiving the Word.

The disciples came to Jesus, asking Him to send them away to buy food. Jesus told His disciples, "You give them something to eat!"

The disciples responded, "All we have is the lunch of this young boy here: five barley rolls and two small fish."

Jesus said, "Bring them to me."

He then took the bread and fish, looked up to heaven, and blessed and broke it and gave it to the disciples. The disciples in turn took it and shared it among the multitude, and they all ate and were filled. Jesus took a young boy's lunch and fed over 5000 people. It was a miracle of increase.

While the disciples were initially focused on their insufficiency, Jesus was focused on sufficiency. The disciples saw the inability of man, while Jesus released the ability of God. When everyone ate and was full, Jesus had them gather up the fragments. There were twelve baskets full of leftovers. He didn't waste anything. Ultimately, God was more than enough.

Miracles of Wisdom

Another miracle of provision in the life of Christ is found in Matthew 17:24-27. When the leaders of the temple at Capernum, Jesus' hometown, asked a question of Peter concerning the temple tax, Jesus responded that they were free.

However, to avoid offense Jesus told Peter to go to the sea and catch the first fish that came. He said, "When you have opened the fish's mouth, you will find a coin: take that and pay the tax for me and you."

While I pastored in rural Colorado, one of my members had miscalculated his prior year earnings and expenses. Initially, his CPA told him that he would owe around $250,000 in tax that year. While he was at church worshipping God, God revealed to him some improvements on a farm that he had bought that could be written off. He asked the CPA, the CPA agreed. The tax was lowered by over 80%! Good things happen when you go to church and get in the presence of God in worship.

Jesus' first miracle was a miracle of provision. In John 2, when Jesus went to a wedding in Cana of Galilee, they ran out of wine. Mary, the mother of Jesus, told the servants, "Do whatever Jesus tells you to do."

There were six water pots that held twenty to thirty gallons each. Jesus told the servants to fill the water pots, and they filled them to the brim. Then Jesus said, "Take some to the governor of the feast."

When the ruler tasted the water that was made wine, he asked "Why didn't you bring the best wine at the beginning of the feast?"

Jesus was ultimately giving a picture of the marriage supper of the Lamb, when we will celebrate His presence forever. In this beginning of miracles, Jesus manifested His glory, and His disciples believed on Him.

Miracles Still Happen

God still provides for us today! Recently, we had a back-to-school bash where we provided supplies for families in need at our church. One mom said, "My daughter needs a purple three ring binder with pockets, but we haven't been able to find them anywhere."

When they looked through the supplies, they found exactly what her daughter needed right on top of the pile. Her daughter saw this as the provision of God. God is really good, and if you look for His goodness, you will find it all around.

The children of Israel lived off of miracles every day for forty years when they went through the wilderness. God provided mana and quail for them six days a week. On the sixth day, they gathered two days' worth. On the seventh day, they rested. Their shoes and clothing never wore out.

When they crossed the Jordan and went back into the promised land, the manna ceased on the morning after they had eaten the corn of the land. They ate of the fruit of the land of Canaan that year (Joshua 5:12).

That meant they had to go to work. They had to plow, to plant, and to harvest.

We can live a blessed life in Christ. There are times we might go from miracle to miracle, but I believe that God wants us to operate in the blessing. I believe that God wants us to be blessed where we don't need miracles every day. I still love the gifts of the Holy Spirit. I love miracles but living in the blessing is awesome.

Provision

It's great when you don't have to have a miracle to pay a $1000 unexpected bill; you can just pay it and go on. Thank God for His Spirit. Thank God for miracles but move into the land of blessing. Move into the land of supernatural increase!

Chapter
Fifteen

THE GOLD FOLLOWS THE GLORY

E arly in the year 2001, Bobby Jean Merck came to our church in Kit Carson and prophesied. Many didn't realize it then, but she was prophesying about the church we were about to plant in Colorado Springs. One of the words that came forth was, "I will glorify the house of my glory."

It is important that we not only individually follow the plan and purpose of God, but that ministries follow the purpose and the plan of God as well.

I have maintained in my thinking the principle that the gold follows the glory. When we walk in the glory—which biblically speaking refers to the purpose, presence, and power of God—I believe there will be provision for the vision (1 Corinthians 15:40-41, 2 Chronicles 5:13-14, John 11:40-44).

Haggai 2:6-9

> *For thus says the Lord of hosts; Yet*
> *once, it is a little while, and I will shake*
> *the heavens, and the earth, and the sea,*
> *and the dry land; And I will shake all*
> *nations, and the desire of all nations*
> *shall come: and I will fill this house with*
> *glory, says the Lord of hosts. The silver*
> *is mine, and the gold is mine, says the*
> *Lord of hosts. The glory of this latter*
> *house shall be greater than of the*
> *former, says the Lord of hosts: and in*
> *this place will I give peace, says the Lord*
> *of hosts.*

Haggai was the prophet of the rebuilding of the temple. The people had been discouraged because they remembered the greatness of the former temple.

Ultimately, God was in the rebuilding of the temple. It spoke of the time when Jesus (the desire of all nations) will come and reign. In His reign, there will be total provision and ultimate peace.

When we walk in the plans and purposes of God, I believe there is provision for us. I have travelled in a number of foreign countries, several of them third world countries. I have met ministers from around the world, and I have seen God provide for them in miraculous ways.

In Nepal, one of the poorest countries in the world, I met ministers who bought property and built houses worth thousands of dollars. It was supernatural. In a place where lack abounds, there was more than enough provision for those who followed God's plans and believed His promises.

I went to Jamaica for a ministry trip right out of High School. There were many people begging and in need. However, I met one individual who went to another island and started a painting business. Then he took the proceeds and bought a car which he used for a taxi.

He was prospering, even though he was surrounded by poverty. This man did not have a victim mentality. He had a victor mentality. He wasn't looking at what he didn't have. He saw opportunity.

What we see is a key to what we receive. When I first moved to Colorado Springs, I was amazed at all of the houses that were selling in the $500,000 plus range (today they would be $800,000 and up).

But I also saw opportunity. In my mind, there wasn't a question of how to make money; it was just a question of what avenue that God wanted us to use to receive His provision.

Prosperous people are not looking at lack. They are not looking at what they don't have. People who are walking in abundance in God's kingdom have learned how to walk in their God-given purpose and how to operate in biblical principles of multiplication.

Provision

I still believe the gold follows the glory. I believe if we find what God wants us to do and follow His plan, there will be more than enough provision to do it. Yes, I am receiving what I believe.

Chapter

Sixteen

GIRLS, GOLD, AND GLORY

W hile I firmly believe the gold follows the glory, there is a balancing truth to the principles of the scriptures. While I attended Bible College, Dr. Lester Sumrall made the statement, "Don't touch the girls, the gold, or the glory."

Several years ago, I restated that in this way, "Beware of sex, money, and power." The wrong attitude toward these things can get one into trouble.

The day after I made that statement, it was revealed that a major leader in the body of Christ had been dealing with a major sex problem. It was a tragedy. In this certain case, I believe there had been multiple opportunities for repentance, but they had not been heeded. God is a God of grace, but we must allow grace to work in and through our lives.

Before I left the house that morning, Barbara said, "Don't ever do that or I'll shoot you." Later that day, a leader at Charis Bible College told me the same thing. Then Andrew Wommack met me and said, "Don't ever do that or I'll shoot you and raise you from the dead." We need accountability in our lives!

Believers need to live pure lives in the areas of sex, money and power. Purity is a virtue in all sexual matters. Biblically speaking, sex outside of marriage is sin, and God is the one who ordained marriage between one man and one woman.

The gold and the glory belong to God. No matter how much God blesses us, we need to keep the attitude that we are stewards of what God has given us.

In the area of finance, 1 Timothy 6 provides insight to a balanced view.

1 Timothy 6:5-8

> *Perverse disputings of men of corrupt minds, and destitute of the truth, supposing that gain is godliness: from such withdraw yourself. But godliness with contentment is great gain. For we brought nothing into this world, and it is certain we can carry nothing out. And having food and clothing let us be content with that.*

Gain is not godliness. One can be rich spiritually and poor physically. It is also possible to be rich physically and poor spiritually. What can one give in exchange for their soul? I have never seen a hearse pull a U-Haul truck!

Be Content

Contentment is a positive thing. Paul wrote his partners in Philippians chapter 4, and right in the middle of a great financial teaching, he said, "I have learned, in whatever state I am, to be content. I know how to be abased and how to abound: everywhere and in all things, I am instructed both to be full and to be hungry, both to abound and to suffer need; I can do all things through Christ who strengthens me" (Philippians 4:11-13).

God wants us to prosper. He also wants us to be content with what He gives us, doing what He called us to do. Part of contentment is revealed in thankfulness. We need to always be grateful for every good thing God has given us.

One aspect of God releasing true wealth in our lives is the attitude of appreciation. We should never cease to be thankful for the good things God has given us spiritually, physically or financially, and we should seek to be stewards of everything that God has gifted us with.

1 Timothy 6:9-12

But they who will be rich fall into temptation and a snare, and into many foolish and hurtful lusts, which drown men in destruction and perdition. For the love of money is the root of all evil: which

> *while some coveted after, they have erred from the faith, and pierced themselves through with many sorrows. But you, man of God, flee these things; and follow after righteousness, godliness, faith, love, patience, meekness. Fight the good fight of faith, lay hold on eternal life, where unto you are called, and have professed a good profession before many witnesses.*

Some in the Christian world have stated that money is the root of all evil. Money is not evil. The *love of money* is the root of all evil. The love of money can cause people to do wicked things. We need to love God, not money. Loving God should help us keep the right attitude toward money.

Be a Good Steward

Ultimately, the right attitude toward money is revealed in stewardship. We should seek to be good stewards of everything God has given us, including time, talents, and treasure.

1 Timothy 6:17-19 (brackets added)

> *Charge them who are rich in this world, that they be not high minded, nor trust in uncertain riches, but in the living God, who gives us richly all things to enjoy; That they do good, that they be rich in good works, ready to distribute, willing to communicate [give]; Laying up in store for themselves a good foundation against*

*the time to come, that they may lay hold
on eternal life.*

Trust in God

Don't trust in money. Trust in God. I just
looked at a twenty-dollar bill and a quarter. Both
of them state, "In God We Trust."

While the United States of America is greatly
in need of revival (which I believe is here now), our
country was founded on godly principles. The
founders of this nation were men and women who
believed and trusted in God. Faith in God is the
only thing that will keep this country from
deteriorating.

When God blesses us, we should not be
arrogant, or trust in our riches. We should trust
in God. He is the one who has given to us richly.
He has given us good things to enjoy.

In response, we should be generous with
others. We need to share the wealth that God has
given us.

Generosity is evidence that we trust in God.
Generosity is evidence that God lives in us.
Generosity lays a good foundation against the
time to come.

Jesus said, "Lay up your treasure in heaven,
where moth nor rust corrupts and where thieves
don't break through and steal" (Matthew 6:20).

Take a lesson from the scripture and Dr. Lester Sumrall. Watch out for the girls, the gold and the glory. Live pure sexually. Don't trust in gold. Trust in God, and always remember that the glory belongs to Him.

Chapter

Seventeen

SEVEN STATEMENTS OF ABUNDANCE

P hilippians 4 is amazing to me. Paul was writing from prison, where he was placed for preaching the Gospel, yet He was rejoicing in the Lord and thanking God and his partners for their kindness to him. Even though his physical condition was challenging at the time, his spiritual state was terrific!

Philippians 4:10-19 (emphasis added)

> *But I rejoiced in the Lord greatly, that now at the last your care of me has flourished again, wherein you were also careful, but you lacked opportunity.* **Not that I speak in respect of want: for I have learned in whatever state I am there with to be content.** *I know how to be abased, and I know how to abound: everywhere and in all things I am instructed both to be full and to be hungry, both to abound and to suffer*

*need. **I can do all things through Christ who strengthens me.** Notwithstanding you have well done, that you did communicate with my affliction. Now you Philippians know also, that in the beginning of the gospel, when I departed from Macedonia, no church communicated with me as concerning giving and receiving, but you only. For even in Thessalonians you sent once and again to my necessity. Not because I desire a gift: but **I desire fruit that may abound to your account**. But **I have all and abound: I am full having received** of Epaphroditus the things which were sent from you, an odor of a sweet smell, a sacrifice acceptable, well pleasing to God. **But my God shall supply all your need according to His riches in glory by Christ Jesus.***

Let's look into Paul's seven statements of abundance found here. These seven statements reveal an attitude of excellence. Our attitude determines our altitude. Having a good attitude is a key to long-term prosperity.

Number One

I do not speak in respect of want. I will not focus on lack. I will focus on abundance. I will talk about what God has given me. I will talk about the goodness of God. I will magnify the provision of God in my life.

A lack mentality led to sin in the garden. Satan tempted Adam and Eve saying, "If you eat of this fruit, you will be like God, knowing good and evil."

Adam and Eve were *already* made in the image of God! The devil succeeded in getting them to focus on what they *didn't* have instead of what they *did* have. Don't let that be your downfall.

Number Two

I have learned to be content. Godliness with contentment is great gain. Believe God to prosper. At the same time, always be thankful for every good thing that God has given you: physically, financially, emotionally, and relationally. Joy and thankfulness are evidence of our faith in God.

Number Three

I can do all things through Christ who strengthens me. Christ is in me and working through me. He is strengthening me. He is enabling me to walk out the purpose and plan of God. He is my victory.

I can do what God has called me to do through the power of Christ in me. Greater is He that is in me that he that is in the world (1 John 4:4). The spirit of Christ in me is greater than the spirit of antichrist in the world.

Whosoever is born of God overcomes the world and this is the victory that overcomes the world, even my faith. Who is he that overcomes the world, but he that believes that Jesus is the Son of God (1 John 5:4-5). Jesus Christ is living in me. I have His life, His nature, and His ability.

This is the Gospel truth for every believer. Knowing this will lead us into His victory. Believers are not lacking in any area. When we know this, we can boldly declare, "I can do all things through Christ who strengthens me."

Christ is in us. He is helping us. Without Him we can do nothing (John 15:5). In every aspect of life, we need to rely on Him and rest in Him. He is the one who ultimately brings us to victory. His overcoming life is in us.

When we rely on Him, we will see His victory manifested in our lives, both now and in eternity. Nothing we are doing, and nothing we have done, is nearly as great as what Christ will do in us. The best is always yet to come in Him.

Number Four

I desire that fruit may abound to your account. I want others to prosper. I want others to come into the abundance that God has for them. One aspect of this is allowing them the opportunity to sow seed in God's kingdom.

If I don't share with others the biblical principles of giving and receiving, and if I don't give them the opportunity to sow seed into the Kingdom of God, I may limit their ability to receive the blessings of God. When we get involved in giving and receiving, in sowing and reaping financially, we are releasing the grace of God in our lives and in the lives of others.

2 Corinthians 9:8

> *And God is able to make all grace abound toward you; that you, always having all sufficiency in all things, may abound to every good work.*

Some grace may only be released when we get involved in the grace of giving. However, when we enter into the grace of giving in the realm of sowing and reaping, it releases all sufficiency in all things! We should desire to give to every good work. Only God can make that a reality.

Number Five

I have all and abound. An attitude of abundance leads to abundance. Paul was in prison for preaching the Gospel, but he was looking at what he had. He wasn't whining and complaining. He wasn't whimpering. He was rejoicing in the goodness of God.

Earlier, in Philippians 4:4, he wrote, "Rejoice in the Lord always and again I say rejoice."

He then went on to say in verse 8, "Whatsoever things are true, honest, just, pure, lovely, whatsoever things are of good report; if there be any virtue, and if there be any praise, think on these things." Paul disciplined his mind to focus on the good. He chose to rejoice. He chose to magnify the positive and to magnify God. He refused to focus on negative things.

I believe that is why, when Paul and Silas were thrown in prison for preaching the Gospel in Acts 16, that God sent His angel and delivered them. After they had been beaten and were in chains for proclaiming the good news, at midnight they prayed and sang praises to God.

God set them free. But rather than run, they stayed around and won the jailor to Christ. Paul and Silas were connected to and controlled by heaven. They were directed by the Holy Spirit. They demonstrated absolute authority in the situation.

When we get our flesh under the control of our spirit and let Jesus live big in us, I believe that we will say with Paul, "I have all and abound." We will be constantly thanking God for what we have and not whimpering about the difficulties in this world. When Paul said that, I believe he was demonstrating Christ-like authority.

When they came to take Jesus to the cross, He could have called ten thousand angels, but He didn't. He willingly went to the cross, to suffer for you and for me, to die for the sins of the world. The soldiers fell back at the power of His Word. But He went to take our punishment and to give us His victory.

Paul demonstrated the victory when He said, "I have all and abound." He was not looking at his outward condition. He was focused on his inward victory.

Number Six

I am full, having received. Accentuate the positive. Focus on the good. Focus on what we have and not what we don't have. Our true condition is our spiritual condition.

The true spiritual condition of every believer is blessed. If you are born again, you are blessed, whether you believe it or not. However, if you don't believe it, you won't see it go to work in your life. If you do believe you are blessed, you will open the door for God to shower you with blessing. A blessed mentality will lead to a blessed life.

If you are born again, if you know Christ as your Savior, you are blessed (Ephesians 1:3; 2 Peter 1:3). Let your spiritual condition determine your state of mind. As you do, you will find that your spiritual condition will affect your physical and natural condition.

God is in us, working through us to will and to do His good pleasure (Philippians 2:13). That is spirit, soul, and body. God works in our spirits. He works through our souls (mind, will and emotions). He will work in our bodies, where we do His good pleasure.

However, if we don't renew our minds, we may never see the victory in our spirits, revealed in our bodies.

Number Seven

My God shall supply all my need according to His riches in glory. Many times we hear this quoted without attention to the context. This is a powerful scriptural truth. When we understand the context, we see what makes it work.

Paul is talking to his partners. He is speaking to those who have partnered with him for years to see the Gospel go forward. He declares to them that God will supply their need according to His riches in glory.

Years ago, I heard someone say, "God will give you what you need and not what you want." The problem with this is that they don't understand the scriptures. Psalm 23:1 declares, "The Lord is my shepherd; *I shall not want.*" Thank God, He not only takes care of needs, He takes care of wants, too.

When we delight ourselves in the Lord, He gives us the desires of our hearts (Psalm 37:4). When we delight ourselves in Him, our desires flow with His desires. He doesn't only take care of our needs, He takes care of our wants.

In Philippians 4:19, Paul takes it further: God supplies all of our needs *according to His riches in glory.* Heaven is not bankrupt. Heaven is rich. God gravels His roads with the purest gold. The foundations of the New Jerusalem are made of the finest stone. The riches and beauty of heaven are unsurpassable. And God supplies our needs according to *His* riches.

There is no lack with God. Heaven is not having a problem paying the light bill. The Lord God and the Lamb are the light of the New Jerusalem. When we get involved in the grace of giving, we put ourselves in a place of receiving the wealth of heaven.

God is able to do exceedingly abundantly above all that we can ask or think, according to the power that works in us (Ephesians 3:20). This is not only for spiritual things, but for natural things as well.

God cares about you. He wants to bless you. He wants to help you. He wants you to proper more than you want to prosper. These are His promises. This is His plan. We need to find out what the scripture says about God, and about us, and boldly declare it.

So let's boldly declare with Paul the Apostle:

I do not speak in respect of want. I have learned in all things to be content. I can do all things through Christ who strengthens me. I desire that fruit may abound to your account. I have all and abound. I am full having received. And My God supplies all my need according to His riches in glory!

Let's move into God's provision for our lives spiritually, emotionally, physically and financially. Let's move into every good thing that God has for us.

Chapter
Eighteen

THE VALUE OF EDUCATION

Many people in the body of Christ want to prosper. However, if the church is going to lead the world in the area of finance, there are certain areas where education is a requirement. If our sons and daughters are going to be doctors, lawyers, and engineers—if they are going to lead major corporations—they will need some education in those fields.

It is not education alone that matters. One of my mentors has an eighth-grade education. He has a tremendous amount of common sense, and he recently told me that he was having a hard time keeping his net worth under ten million dollars.

But each of us are gifted in different ways, and in certain fields, education is required. For example, my doctor is a spirit-filled Christian, and his faith is contagious. However, it took an education for him to get his position.

What is the best education? Should everyone home school, or should everyone go to Christian school? What about public school? Is it a sin to put your children in public school?

The reason I am asking these questions is because of attitudes that I see in the body of Christ. Recently, at a meeting with some leaders in my church, one of the men who has small children said, "I'm just going to keep my children out of public education." That may be a good answer for some, but I do not believe that one size fits all.

While home school may be the best option for some, Christian school may be a better for others, and public education may be the best option for some. We all need to do what is best for our children, and we need to be realistic about it.

I was the salutatorian of my High School class. I was the valedictorian of my Bible School class. And I chose to put my children in public school.

Decisions for our children should never be made out of fear. We need to teach them to develop their gifts. Proverbs 22:6 says, "Train up a child in the way he should go and when he his old, he will not depart from it." The way he should go is referring to their personal gifts and talents. Our children need training according to their God-given abilities.

I have friends I respect who put their children in Christian School, and some other good friends who home schooled their children. But the fact is, we as parents need to see that our children have a good education and the tools necessary to be successful in life. Whether God has called them to ministry or into the realm of business, they will need good training.

In his book, *The Midas Touch*, Dr. Kenneth E. Hagin shared some really practical insight in this area. He said that if our children are going to be leaders in a certain industry, they must have the educational background to do it.

I am a realist. I don't like people who have the very best education that money can buy telling people certain things because that is what they want to hear. I want to know what works. I want to be honest about the situation.

The church is to be the light of the world and the salt of the earth. We need to let our light shine brightly. There are times when we are called to "come out from among them and be separate," and there are times when we are called "not to be taken out of the world, but to be kept from the evil of it" (2 Corinthians 6:14-18, John 17:15).

We all need to be set apart from the world by the Word. When we are set apart by the Word, then we can be sent to the world. The world needs to see the church shining as a light, shining bright and shining strong. If we go hide in a hole somewhere and wonder what is happening, we will never be that light (John 17:15-18).

We are a spirit, soul, and body. Spiritually speaking, we need to teach our children to love God.

Emotionally speaking, we need to love our children and teach them to love their families. Academically speaking, we need to see that they have the education they need to fulfill their God-given talents.

Financially speaking, we need to teach them a practical trade. Physically speaking, we need to teach them to take care of their bodies. I was in sports in Junior High and High School, and it was good for me. All of my boys were in sports, and it was good for them, too.

Many times, in the church, we just focus on the spiritual being. Our spirit is one part of us, but it is not the whole person. We need to think about the whole person. We need to think about spirit, soul, and body.

I want my children to lead, not only in the spiritual arena, but in the business arena as well, and they are. However, it took an education for them to move into the areas that God called them to. Even though each of my boys chose to go to secular colleges, where they could best be educated for the fields of their choosing, they did not compromise their faith.

Chapter

Nineteen

ABOUNDING IN THE BLESSING

J esus said, "It is more blessed to give than to receive" (Acts 20:35). If we are going to abound in the blessing, we must get involved in giving.

Proverbs 3:9-10

Honor the LORD with your substance, and with the firstfruits of all your increase: So your barns will be filled with plenty, and your presses will burst out with new wine.

God wants to bring increase and supernatural blessing into our lives. However, for His promises in the area of financial increase to work, we need to begin to sow into His kingdom.

In the natural, if we don't sow a seed, we cannot receive a harvest, and in the spiritual, it works much the same way.

Proverbs 11:24-25 (NKJV)

> *There is one who scatters, yet increases more; And there is one who withholds more than is right, But it leads to poverty. The generous soul will be made rich, And he who waters will also be watered himself.*

There has been a Biblical principle in existence since Genesis 8:22, and it is called sowing and reaping, or seedtime and harvest. As long as the earth remains, there will be sowing and reaping, seed time and harvest, summer and winter, cold and heat. There will be provision on the earth for the people on the earth as long as the earth is here (Genesis 8:22).

If we want to get a harvest, we must sow a seed. If we want a harvest financially, we need to get involved in sowing. Paul encourages this aspect of the gospel in 2 Corinthians 8-9.

In the first five verses of 2 Corinthians 8, Paul writes the believers and encourages them to take lessons from the Macedonian church. The Macedonians were a tremendous example in giving. It was not because of easy circumstances that they were givers; in fact, it was in spite of circumstances that they were giving.

In their trouble, the Amplified Bible says that they "Overflowed in lavish generosity," and they did it voluntarily. No one was twisting their arms to provoke them to give. This church was a generous (liberal) church. They gave financially because they had first given themselves to the Lord spiritually.

Isaiah 32:8 is a promise to those who are generous. It says, "The liberal devises liberal things; and by liberal things shall he stand." The word for liberal here means generous.

Two things are evident is this scripture. First, generous people devise (come up with) generous things. Second, by generous things we stand. God gives seed to sowers, therefore, if you want more seed, keep sowing (giving). When we sow, our seed creates a harvest. By generous things we stand.

The Generous are Blessed

Proverbs 22:9 says that those who have a bountiful (or generous) eye will be blessed. They see where they can give. When we are generous, I believe we live under an open heaven.

Next to our family farm where I grew up, we had neighbors who lived this out. I remember them talking about how a young child could not drink cow's milk, so they gave the family goat's milk away at no charge. They were believers, and they were generous.

This family was unconventional. One summer they planted the seed cleanings instead of regular seed. Almost no one would do that.

That summer, most of the wheat near our farm was destroyed by hail. But our neighbors let their sheep pasture off the wheat and weeds from the seed cleanings and made a good profit when everyone else around them lost money.

One of my financial mentors, Aubrey Shotton, who lived Southwest of Eads, Colorado, was raised in a traditional church. But when he heard the word about freedom from the curse, he took it literally.

One summer there was a plague of grasshoppers. Everyone was spraying their crops, but not Aubrey. He went to his field and cursed the grasshoppers and believed God.

Aubrey custom farmed right next to his field. The person who he custom farmed for demanded that Aubrey have the custom crops sprayed. Aubrey obeyed and sprayed those crops yet did not spray his own. He just continued to believe God.

At harvest time, Aubrey's field that was just next to the sprayed crops actually yielded a greater harvest! Aubrey saved thousands of dollars. He was a giver. These are just a couple examples of the blessing of God on generous people.

My sons are all generous givers, and blessings continually overtake them.

Just today, Aaron was looking for some desks on Craigslist for the church. During his search, he found a small, high-end Ethan Allen desk that we wouldn't use for the church. When he contacted the sellers, they gave it to his son Fisher and delivered it for free!

My son Andrew was leaving a job for a better one God had opened up. He asked me to pray for him. He said, "They just walk some people out, box up their stuff and give them their last check."

Andrew purposely told his former employer that he was leaving the week before the bonuses and extra benefits came out. His boss asked, "Didn't you know that those bonuses and profit sharing were coming out next week?"

Andrew replied in the affirmative. His boss then asked, "Then why did you tell us that you were going to leave this week?"

Andrew said, "I thought that was the right thing to do." His boss then gave him the full profit sharing and bonus. Not only did he give Andrew a $28,000 dollar bonus when he was leaving the company, he also told him that he could work for them in the future anytime he wanted to. That's what I call blessed going out!

Andrew's new company gave him $20,000 per year more than he had asked for and a higher position. That is blessed coming in! We can be blessed going out and coming in. We need to live generously and live with integrity!

Andrew believes that he has a gift to give. He is very generous. He has addicted himself to giving, and God is supporting his habit.

In 2 Corinthians 8, Paul used the Macedonians as examples in giving. He said they gave as much as they possibly could.

This generosity reflected the condition of their hearts.

Paul encouraged the Corinthians to get involved in the grace of giving. He implored them to follow the Macedonian example. He said, "You abound in faith, knowledge, diligence and love, so why not get involved in giving too?" Furthermore, Paul implied that talk is cheap.

Talk is Cheap

In his apostolic leadership, Paul told them to look at the example of Jesus. Jesus was ultimately the greatest giver. He gave the greatest of all gifts— His own life. God received the greatest harvest in giving us Jesus, the salvation of all who will believe!

When Paul encouraged them to start sowing, he told them essentially that God is not concerned about what you don't have. If you make up your mind to be a giver, God will see that you have seed to sow.

Kenneth Copeland started in sowing and reaping by giving a pencil, and now he is one of the wealthiest ministers of the Gospel in the world. Kenneth personally funds all the ministers on his television channel.

When I checked out what it would cost to have a channel on Dish Network, it was $5 million per year. And that's just the beginning cost without the expense of running it! You should never criticize a person's harvest until you have seen their seed!

In 2 Corinthians 8, Paul explained that he had sent Titus to help administrate the gift. As we grow, we need help in administering what God has given us or we can get sloppy in stewardship. When they were good stewards of what God had given them, it led to abundance (2 Corinthians 8:20).

Finally, Paul said, "Don't blame us for the abundance administered by us." It's important that we don't assign blame to ministries that are blessed with abundance. If we do, we may limit our ability to receive what God wants to bring to us!

If we are going to administrate well what God has given us, honesty is a must and diligence is required. Stewarding well is a lifelong practice. When we stay at it, it leads to super blessing!

To abound in the blessing, we must allow grace to reign big in the area of giving and receiving. 2 Corinthians 9:8 declares, "God is able to make all grace abound toward you; that you, always having all sufficiency in all things, may abound to every good work." I believe if we live in light of this scripture, we can live in unlimited grace.

In the Old Testament, when Israel gathered their harvest, they were to leave the corners of the fields for the poor (Leviticus 23:22). As this became a practice, it was believed that God enlarged their borders.

There are numerous areas where I have been very generous with people. Some of them have taken advantage of me. However, in the end, when I gave generously, I sowed it as a seed, and God has caused that seed to come up in my field! When you are a generous person, some may take advantage, but God sees your heart. So, sow it as a seed and believe God for the harvest. Don't get bitter!

When we practice the principles of sowing and reaping in 2 Corinthians 8-9, and administrate stewardship well, it will lead to thanksgiving.

2 Corinthians 9:11

> *Being enriched in every thing to all bountifulness, which causes through us thanksgiving to God.*

The final result of generous giving, good stewardship, and good administration is that it brings thanks to God. Ultimately, we thank God for His unspeakable gift of Jesus. Giving is a reflection of the grace of Jesus in our lives.

Chapter

Twenty

WORSHIPPING GOD
THROUGH GIVING

R ecently, my daughter-in-law, Heather, shared on three different aspects of giving.

First, she talked about tithing. She shared that as a young believer, she gave out of fear, knowing that the Old Testament declared a curse on those who did not tithe, and a blessing on those who do (Malachi 3:8-10).

Second, she shared on the principle of sowing and reaping, which is the primary thing that I have shared and teach concerning giving. I believe that sowing and reaping is a perpetual principle that has been on the earth since Genesis and will continue as long as the earth remains (Genesis 8:22).

The third aspect that she shared was on worshipping God though our giving.

When Heather shared this, something jumped in my heart. I knew scripturally the aspect of worshipping through giving. But it just became a revelation to me.

Heather is an amazing giver, and I know that this principle of worship is the motivation behind her generosity.

In Deuteronomy 26, God gave the children of Israel instructions on tithes and offerings. The first thing that He said was to take the first of anything God gives you and bring it where God has placed His name.

Where does God place His name today? The great commission in Mark 16:15-18 gives us some insight: "In my name they shall cast out devils; they shall speak with new tongues... they shall lay hands on the sick and they shall recover."

God puts his name where people are being saved, healed, delivered and filled with the Holy Ghost. God puts His name where there is an ongoing move of the Holy Spirit. We should worship God with our money by giving it where God places His Name.

The second thing He said was to take your offering to the priest. Jesus is the Great High Priest of the New Testament, and He receives our offerings today (Hebrews 7).

The third thing they did was thank God for His goodness. They were instructed to thank God for

His deliverance and His Provision. They were asked to rejoice in what God had given to them and what He had done for them.

Finally, they were to confess that they had brought the holy things to the Lord and to ask for, and thank Him for, the blessing He had placed on them.

We need to continually be thankful for every good thing God has given us and trust Him for His blessing. Believers are to worship God with their money.

Two instances in the life of Jesus stand out in the aspect of worshipping God with our money. One of them is the widow who gave two mites. The other one is the woman who broke her alabaster box and poured the contents on Jesus. Both of these instances show the heart of true worship.

Mark 12:41-44

> *And Jesus sat over against the treasury, and watched how the people cast money into the treasury: and many who were rich cast in much. And there came a certain poor widow, and she threw in two mites, which make a farthing. And he called unto him his disciples and said to them, Truly I say to you, That this poor widow has cast more in, than all they who have cast into the treasury: For all they did cast in of their abundance; but she of her want did cast in all that she had, even all her living.*

This woman gave about two cents in today's terms in the offering, yet Jesus said she gave more than those who had probably put in thousands of dollars. One of the principles Jesus was teaching is that it's not the total amount given that matters. Rather, it is the percentage given that is most important.

This is the heart of true worship. This woman gave everything that she had. She completely trusted God in her giving. I believe that if God has our heart, it will show up in our bank account. If God has our heart, He will have our money. What we do with money is just an outward sign of the position of our heart.

Mark 14:3-9

> *And being in Bethany in the house of Simon the leper, as He sat at meat, there came a woman having an alabaster box of ointment of spikenard very precious; and she broke the box, and poured it on His head. And there were some who had indignation within themselves, and said, Why was this waste of the ointment made? For it might have been sold for more than three hundred pence, and have been given to the poor. And they murmured against her. And Jesus said, Let her alone; why do you trouble her? She has worked a good work on me. For you have the poor with you always, and whenever you want, you may do them good: but me you will not always have. She has done what she could: she has*

come beforehand to anoint my body for burial. Truly I say to you, Wherever this gospel will be preached throughout the whole world, this thing that she has done shall be spoken of for a memorial of her.

What an amazing act of generosity. This dear woman's gift was approximately the value of one year's salary! While the religious criticized this gift as waste, Jesus praised the woman for her act of worship.

Not only was she bringing a gift, but her gift told the story that she had completely given her heart to Christ. The gift anointed Him prior to his crucifixion and burial. It was an act of total surrender and heartfelt worship. Jesus said that wherever the Gospel would be preached, this would be a memorial of her.

I believe two things will happen when we get a revelation of giving as worship. First of all, our giving will go to a completely different level. Second, we will take pleasure in giving like never before!

Chapter

Twenty-One

BREAKING THE
POVERTY MENTALITY

Our neighbors on a farm close to where I grew up had a business card that said, "We've done so much with so little for so long, we can almost do anything with nothing."

That may be a somewhat true statement, but it reeks of poverty. I used to read jokes in farm papers that deemed most agricultural people as poor. When I renewed my mind, I quit reading those jokes, and I had to get rid of a whole bunch of unscriptural and ungodly preconceived ideas. Having a poverty mentality is unscriptural, and it is ungodly!

Part of breaking this poverty mentality came to me when I heard and believed the truth that God wants us to prosper. That began in 1978. But a greater aspect of breaking it came in 1998, when I went to the Mark Hankins meeting in Denver and he challenged my religion by talking about buying his wife a new luxury car.

Religious thinking is carnal mindedness. The carnal mind is an enemy of God. It is not subject to the law of God. Poor thinking is not holy!

The problem with poor thinking is that it will keep you poor. My grandmother told me that I should not be a preacher because preachers were poor people. That is carnal. Although in some cases it may be true, it is not spiritual thinking.

My wife also had family members who initially discouraged her about going into the ministry because they felt we would be poor. When we first went into the ministry, there was a man who told Barbara that we should live in a tent to prove that we were holy. That is one of the dumbest things I have ever heard.

That man was living in a nice ranch house when he told Barbara that. In a few years, he lost his job and that house. He ended up living in a shack. He had multiple problems with his wife and his children. He was one of the most legalistic people I have ever known, and it did not work out well.

I believe he could have repented. He could have changed his mind and had different results. But some people like to hold on to their legalistic religion.

I knew of a church one time that got mad at their pastor for buying a roll of stamps to send cards to the visitors. That is terrible. This was a holiness church. They were all into hair length, dress length, and shirt sleeve length. It was all about outward holiness. Some of those things have some wisdom, but in this case, their thinking about money was despicable!

Soon after those Mark Hankins meetings in 1998, I spent several months praying and personalizing these three portions of scripture. It did something to me, through me, and for me. The three scripture passages that I prayed were Deuteronomy 28:1-14, Psalm 112:1-10 and Psalm 115:9-16.

I prayed them and personalized them for three to six months, five to seven days per week. When I did that, I began to think bigger and better! If you are having problems in the area of financial increase, I challenge you to do the same thing I did. God is no respecter of persons!

One of the greatest cures for a poverty mentality is super generous giving. When you get used to giving large amounts of money on a regular basis, it just changes the way you think. Things that seemed hard don't seem to be such a stretch.

For me it hasn't been much of a problem to expand my thinking in the area of giving. My challenge is in the area of spending, especially when it comes to personal things. But gradually the chains are breaking, and I am able to live, enjoy, and share those blessings with my family and others.

Chapter

Twenty-Two

PROSPERITY FROM GENESIS TO REVELATION

P rosperity is a biblical thing. We can see it all through the scriptures. If you believe the Bible, you believe that it is God's will and plan for people to prosper.

In Genesis, God created mankind. He blessed them. He gave them authority, and He gave them ability. He gave them every seed that reproduces, and He gave them animals that have life and reproduce. He gave humanity authority, and He gave them ability (Genesis 1:26-31).

Genesis also reveals that Abraham had a covenant of blessing. God blessed him and he became rich (Genesis 12:1-3; 13:2; 15:1-6; 17:1-2; 24:35).

Abraham's seed was blessed, too. Isaac sowed in the land in the time of famine and reaped a hundredfold. He had great possessions, and the Philistines envied him (Genesis 26:12-14).

Jacob got involved in tithing and became very wealthy (Genesis 28:22; Genesis 32:5).

Joseph carried on the blessing. Joseph was blessed in his father's house, in Potiphar's house, in the prison house, and as prime minister of Egypt. He put Israel in Goshen, the best of the land (Genesis 39:3-5; 47:6).

In the book of Exodus, Israel left Egypt. When they left, they took the silver, the gold, and the livestock. They took the wealth of Egypt with them (Psalm 105:37).

In Leviticus, laws were made for Israel's good. When they followed the principles of the scripture, they found great blessing. Leaving the corners of the fields for the poor is just one example (Leviticus 23:22). It has been said that when they left the corners of their fields for the poor, God enlarged their borders.

In Numbers, Balaam came to curse Israel and ultimately blessed them three times (Numbers 23:19-23).

In Deuteronomy, God told the children of Israel to remember Him when they took possession of the cities they didn't build, the orchards they didn't plant, and the houses filled with good things that they didn't fill (Deuteronomy 6-8). He also gave them the covenant of blessing and the curse in Deuteronomy 28. He promised to bless them for choosing life in Deuteronomy 30:15-19.

In Joshua, Joshua took the children of Israel into the promised land and divided the inheritance among them. They were a very blessed and prosperous people.

Caleb took the mountain where the biggest giants and best fruit were (Joshua 14:10-15).

In Judges, Gideon got the revelation that God is Jehovah Shalom. He is the Lord our peace and our provider. Gideon led the children of Israel to take back their inheritance from their enemies (Judges 6:24).

In the book of Ruth, we see Boaz, the family member with the right of redemption. He is a type of Christ. Ruth believed and saw great grace and blessing. Boaz purchased Ruth and brought her into a wealthy place of living where she became great grandmother to King David. Boaz provided for and protected Ruth before she ever knew him, just as Christ has provided for and protected us before we ever knew Him. Part of redemption is provision (Ruth 2:8-12).

In 1 Samuel 9:22, when Samuel was about to anoint Saul to be the first king of Israel, Samuel took Saul and his servants into his parlor (kitchen) where he had about thirty people seated. It must have been some kitchen!

In 2 Samuel 24:24, David purchased the threshing floor and sacrifices from Arunah for an offering to the Lord for fifty shekels of silver, almost two times the price of a slave.

In 1 Kings 3:12-13, God promised to give Solomon riches and honor like none before him, because he asked for wisdom to fulfill his calling. Solomon made silver so abundant in Israel that they piled it in the streets and gave up trying to count it.

In 2 Kings 4:1-6, a widow woman asked the prophet Elisha what to do because her husband was a prophet and died and left her in debt. The creditor was coming to take her sons as slaves. She received a miracle of increase, paid the debt, and lived with her sons on the overflow!

In 1 Chronicles, David took four hundred men who were in debt, distressed, and discontented. He became king over all of Israel. At the end of his life, David gave a personal offering of over $4 billion in today's currency for the building of the future temple by Solomon. Following his offering, his mighty men—the former four hundred in debt, distressed, and discontented—gave an offering of over $5 billion! David was a man after God's own heart (1 Chronicles 29:1-21).

In 2 Chronicles 9:1-12, the Queen of Sheba came seeking Solomon's wisdom and was overwhelmed by it. She gave him gold in abundance and precious stones. In 2 Chronicles 9:24, Solomon surpassed all the kings of the earth in riches and wisdom.

In 2 Chronicles 20, Israel faced a battle with insurmountable odds. In the midst of the challenge, King Jehoshaphat declared, "Believe in the Lord your God, and you will be established;

believe His prophets, so shall you prosper" (v 20). Israel won a stunning victory that day. In 2 Chronicles 31:4-10, King Hezekiah received an offering for the restoration of worship and had plenty left over.

Ezra prophesied of the rebuilding of the temple and the leaders gave 8,133 ounces of gold (about $1.5 million) and 5000 pounds of silver (just shy of $2 million) for the work (Ezra 2:69).

Nehemiah received no wages for being the governor of Jerusalem for twelve years. During the rebuilding of the wall, he fed over one hundred fifty people a day at his own expense. They butchered one ox and six choice sheep just to feed the people every day (Nehemiah 5:14-19). Nehemiah was a prosperous man.

Esther was a Jewish orphan who became the queen of the Media-Persian Empire, the largest empire to in the history of humanity. At the end of the book, Mordecai, Esther's uncle, became the governor, sought the wealth of God's people, and spoke peace to the seed of the Jews. Esther was given the house of Haman, who had paid a $165 million bribe to the king to destroy the Jews (Esther 3:9; 8:7; 10:1-3.)

Job was attacked by satan and lost his health, his wealth, and his family. In the end, he forgave his friends, found grace, and God restored his family and his wealth (Job 42:12).

Job started out as the richest man in all the east and ended up with twice as much. He also had seven sons and three daughters. He lived for one hundred forty more years and saw his sons and daughters for four generations (Job 42:13-17).

Prosperity in the Poetic Books

Psalms is full of prosperity promises!

Psalm 5:12

> *For you, O LORD, will bless the righteous; with favor you will compass him as with a shield.*

Psalm 23:1

> *The LORD is my shepherd; I shall not want.*

Psalm 23:5

> *You prepare a table before me in the presence of my enemies: you anoint my head with oil; my cup runs over.*

Psalm 34:10

> *...They who seek the LORD shall not want any good thing.*

Psalm 35:27

> *Let them shout for joy, and be glad, who favor my righteous cause: yes, let them say continually, Let the LORD be magnified, who has pleasure in the prosperity of his servant.*

Psalm 37:25

*I have been young, and now I am old;
yet I have not seen the righteous forsaken, nor his seed begging bread.*

Psalm 37:26

...His seed is blessed.

Psalm 66:12

*...We went through fire and through
water: but you brought us out into a
wealthy place.*

Psalm 67:5-6

*Let the people praise you...Then the
earth shall yield her increase; and God,
even our own God, shall bless us.*

Psalm 68:19

*Blessed be the Lord, who daily loads us
with benefits, even the God of our
salvation. Selah*

Psalm 103:5

*Who satisfies your mouth with good
things so that your youth is renewed like
the eagle's.*

Psalm 105:24

*He increased his people greatly and
made them stronger than their enemies.*

Psalm 105:37 (brackets added for clarity)

He brought them forth also with silver and gold: and there was not one feeble [poor, sick)] person among their tribes [families].

Psalm 107:38

He blesses them also, so that they are multiplied greatly; and suffers not their cattle to decrease.

Psalm 112:2-3

His seed shall be mighty on the earth: the generation of the upright shall be blessed. Wealth and riches shall be in his house: and his righteousness endures forever.

Psalm 115:12-15

The LORD has been mindful of us: He will bless us; He will bless the house of Israel; He will bless the house of Aaron. He will bless those who fear the LORD, both small and great. The LORD will increase you more and more, you and your children.

Psalm 122:6-7

Pray for the peace of Jerusalem: they shall prosper who love you. Peace be in your walls, and prosperity in your palaces.

Psalm 133:3

...There the Lord commands His bless-
ing, even life for evermore.

Psalm 145:16

You open your hand, and satisfy the
desire of every living thing.

These verses from Psalms are just the
beginning. There are actually many more!

Proverbs 8:21

That I may cause those who love me to
inherit substance; and I will fill their
treasures.

Proverbs 10:22

The blessing of the LORD makes rich, and
He adds no sorrow with it.

Proverbs 11:24-25

There are those who scatter, and yet
increases; and there are those who
withhold more than is sufficient, but it
tends to poverty. The liberal soul shall
be made fat: and he who waters others
shall be watered himself.

Proverbs 13:22

A good man leaves an inheritance to his
children's children: and the wealth of
the sinner is laid up for the just.

Proverbs 14:4

Where no oxen are, the crib is clean: but much increase is by the strength of the ox.

Proverbs 14:23

In all work there is profit: but the talk of the lips tends to poverty.

Proverbs 19:14

House and riches are the inheritance of fathers...

Proverbs 21:20

There is treasure to be desired and oil in the dwelling of the wise; but a foolish man spends it up.

These are only a few in the Proverbs. Live by Proverbs and you will prosper!

Ecclesiastes 5:19

Every man also to whom God has given riches and wealth, and has given him power to eat thereof, and to take his portion, and to rejoice in his labor; this is the gift of God.

Song of Solomon 3:6-11 speaks of the coming of the king.

Song of Solomon 3:10

He made the pillars thereof of silver, the bottom thereof of gold, the covering of it

*of purple, the midst thereof being paved
with love, for the daughters of Jerusalem.*

Ultimately, Jesus will come as our King, and
He will reign in wealth and power.

Prosperity in the Prophetic Books

Isaiah also has many promises of the coming
prosperity of God's people. Isaiah 54 talks of the
blessing of the New Covenant:

Isaiah 54:11-12

*...I will lay your stones with fair colors,
and lay your foundations with sap-
phires. And I will make your windows of
agates, and your gates of carbuncles,
and all your borders of pleasant stones.*

Isaiah 61:7 talks about the future glory of the
coming kingdom and the people of God. It says,
*"For your shame you shall have double; and for
confusion they shall rejoice in their portion:
therefore in their land they shall possess the
double: everlasting joy shall be to them."*

Isaiah 1:19 is an outright promise of prosperity:
*"If you are willing and obedient you will eat the
good of the land."*

Jeremiah 33:9

*And it shall be to me a name of joy, a
praise and an honor before all the nations of the earth, which shall hear all*

the good that I do unto them: and they shall fear and tremble for all the goodness and for all the prosperity that I procure to it.

Lamentations 4:2

The precious sons of Zion, comparable to fine gold, how are they esteemed as earthen pitchers, the work of the hands of the potter.

Yes, we are God's inheritance; He treasures us!

Ezekiel saw the coming kingdom. He saw the temple and the eastern gate. In Ezekiel 47:9 He saw a great revival. He saw a river that made everything live that it touched. Everyone who came to the water was healed. This is ultimate prosperity: receiving life from the river of life.

In Ezekiel 16:13 He saw those who God had covenant with, and he said, *"You were decked with gold and silver; and your clothes were of fine linen, and silk, and broidered work; you did eat fine flour, and honey, and oil: and you were exceeding beautiful, and you did prosper into a kingdom."*

Daniel received tremendous prosperity through the revelation God gave him. He ruled in three world empires under four different kings. When Daniel predicted the fall of the Babylonian empire, Belshazzar clothed him with scarlet, and put a chain of gold on his neck, making him the third ruler in the kingdom (Daniel 5:29).

Hosea showed that the best prosperity is through a relationship of love that God gives us. God declared in Hosea 2:8, *"For she did not know that I gave her corn, and wine, and oil, and multiplied her silver and gold, which they prepared for Baal."* Even when people don't know Him, all good ultimately comes from God.

Joel predicted the blessing of prosperity that comes from the outpouring of the Spirit. In Joel 2:24, he wrote that the floors will be full of wheat, and the vats will overflow with new wine. Verse twenty-five continues, *"I will restore."*

Amos prophesied of the impending judgment of God. But he ended with a word of hope in Amos 9:13-15. Verse 13 promises, *"The plowman shall overtake the reaper, and the treader of grapes him who sows seed; and the mountains shall drop sweet wine, and all the hills shall melt."*

Sowing and reaping will increase in intensity and in velocity in the last days! The harvest from our seed sown will come more quickly than in former times.

My son Aaron was instructed by the Holy Spirit to increase a missions offering by ten times. Within ten minutes of his gift, he got a notification from his online business that he had sold a product. His seed was returned within ten minutes! That is a supernatural return.

Obadiah 17 says, *"But on mount Zion shall be deliverance, and there shall be holiness; and the house of Jacob shall possess their possessions."*

Wickedness will be judged in the last days, but the church and Israel will have freedom and possess the promises. Jesus came to redeem us from all that Adam lost, including physical possessions.

Jonah 4:11

> *And should I not spare Nineveh, that great city, wherein are more than 120,000 people who cannot discern between their right hand and their left hand; and also much cattle?*

Jonah was angry with God when the people of Nineveh repented in response to his preaching. God's reply to Jonah proves that he cares for people *and* their possessions.

Micah 4:13

> *Arise and thresh, O daughter of Zion: for I will make your horn iron, and I will make your hooves brass: and you shall beat in pieces many people: and I will consecrate their gain to the LORD, and their substance to the LORD of the whole earth.*

Micah prophesied of the victory of the people of God. When they win the victory, God will consecrate their gain (prosperity) to Himself and their substance (wealth) to the Lord of the whole earth (Jesus).

Nahum is written about the impending judgment of Nineveh for rejecting the mercy of

God. In the middle of judgment, God declares His goodness. God will protect and bless those who trust in Him.

Nahum 1:7

> *The LORD is good, a strong hold in the day of trouble; and He knows those who trust in Him.*

Habakkuk writes his burden, vision and prayer. His burden was to cry out, "Why do the wicked overcome the righteous?"

His vision comes from Habakkuk 2:11: *"For the stone shall cry out of the wall, and the beam out of timber shall answer it."* He saw Jesus, the stone that the builders rejected, and he saw the cross, God's ultimate provision for humanity.

Finally, Habakkuk chose to rejoice in the Lord and joy in the God of his salvation, no matter what the physical outcome (3:18).

Zephaniah declares God's judgment on the wicked. However, in the middle of judgment, He shows promises of peace and provision to his people.

Zephaniah 2:9

> *Therefore as I live, says the LORD of Hosts, the God of Israel, Surely Moab shall be as Sodom, and the children of Ammon as Gomorrah, even the breeding of nettles, and saltpits, and a perpetual desolation: the residue of my people*

shall spoil them, and the remnant of my people shall possess them.

Zephaniah 3:13

The remnant of Israel shall not do iniquity, nor speak lies; neither shall a deceitful tongue be found in their mouth: for they shall feed and lie down, and none shall make them afraid.

Haggai declares the glory and wealth of the coming kingdom of our Lord.

Haggai 2:7-9

And I will shake all nations, and the desire of all nations shall come: and I will fill this house with glory, says the LORD of hosts.

The silver is mine, and the gold is mine, says the LORD of hosts. The glory of this latter house shall be greater than the former, says the LORD of hosts: and in this place will I give peace, says the LORD of hosts.

Zechariah prophesied of the future prosperity of the people of God.

Zechariah 8:12

For the seed shall be prosperous; the vine shall give her fruit, and the ground shall give her increase, and the heavens shall give their dew; and I will cause the remnant of this people to possess all these things.

Malachi declares a promise of prosperity to those who are in covenant with God through giving and receiving.

Malachi 3:10-12

Bring all the tithes into the storehouse, that there may be meat in my house, and prove me now in it, says the LORD of hosts, if I will not open you the windows of heaven, and pour you out a blessing, that there will not be room enough to receive it. And I will rebuke the devourer for your sakes, and he shall not destroy the fruits of your ground; neither shall your vine cast her fruit before the time in the field, says the LORD of hosts. And all nations shall call you blessed: for you shall be a delightsome land, says the LORD of hosts.

I believe we live under an open heaven today because of the work of Christ in His death, burial and resurrection. Christ has taken our curse and left us only the blessing!

Prosperity in the New Covenant

Matthew 6:33

But seek ye first the kingdom of God, and His righteousness; and all these things shall be added to you.

Matthew 25:21

...Well done, you good and faithful servant: you have been faithful over a few things, I will make you ruler over many things: enter into the joy of your Lord.

Mark 10:29-30

And Jesus answered and said, Truly I say to you, There is no man who has left house, or brothers, or sisters, or father, or mother, or wife, or children, or lands for my sake, and the gospel's, But he shall receive a hundredfold now in this time, houses, and brothers, and sisters, and mothers, and children, and lands, with persecutions; and in the world to come eternal life.

Luke 12:30-32

For all these things do the nations of the world seek after: and your Father knows that you have need of these things. But rather seek the kingdom of God; and all these things shall be added to you. Fear not, little flock; for it is your Father's good pleasure to give you the kingdom.

Jesus' first miracle was a miracle of provision. In John 2:1-11, Jesus worked his first miracle by blessing the wedding at Cana. He turned water into wine: about one hundred fifty gallons of it! And it wasn't just regular wine. The governor of the feast said it was the best wine! Jesus manifested His glory and His disciples believed on Him.

In John 6:1-14, Jesus took a little boy's lunch and fed more than 5000 people. When He was done, there were still twelve baskets full of leftovers. Both were miracles of more than enough.

In Acts 11:27-30, Agabus warned of a great famine in all of their world. The disciples, hearing of the dilemma, according to their ability, sent relief by the hands of Barnabas and Saul. I believe that the body of Christ collectively has the power to eliminate starvation from the world.

Romans 1:16 says that the Gospel is the power of God to salvation—*soteria* in the Greek. The definition includes forgiveness, healing, prosperity, peace and freedom. Provision is part of salvation at its very root.

Romans 4:13-16 reveals that the promise made to the seed of Abraham was by grace through faith. Part of that promise included physical prosperity.

Romans 10:12, 15

> *For there is no difference between the Jew and the Greek: for the same Lord over all is rich unto all who call upon Him... How beautiful are the feet of them who preach the gospel of peace, and bring glad tidings of good things!*

The good things of the Gospel include God's promises of provision.

1 Corinthians 16:2

Upon the first day of the week let every one of you lay by him in store, as God has prospered him, that there be no gatherings when I come.

2 Corinthians 8:9

For you know the grace of our Lord Jesus Christ, that, though He was rich, yet for your sakes He became poor, that you through His poverty might be rich.

2 Corinthians 9:6-11

But this I say, He who sows sparingly shall reap also sparingly; and he who sows bountifully shall reap also bountifully. Every man according as he purposes in his heart, so let him give; not grudgingly, or of necessity: for God loves a cheerful giver. And God is able to make all grace abound to you; that you, always having all sufficiency in all things, may abound to every good work: (As it is written, He has dispersed abroad; he has given to the poor: his righteousness remains forever. Now He who ministers seed to the sower both minister bread for your food, and multiply your seed sown, and increase the fruits of your righteousness;) Being enriched in every thing to all bountifulness, which causes through us thanksgiving to God.

Galatians 3:8-9

...Preached before the gospel to Abraham, saying, In you shall all nations be blessed. So then those who are of faith are blessed with faithful (believing) Abraham.

Galatians 3:13-14 (brackets added)

Christ has redeemed us from the curse of the law [including poverty] *being made a curse for us: for it is written Cursed is every one who hangs on a tree: That the blessing of Abraham might come on the Gentiles through Jesus Christ; that we might receive the promise of the Spirit through faith.*

Galatians 3:29

If you are Christ's, then you are Abraham's seed, and heirs according to the promise.

Ephesians 1:3

...Who has blessed us with all spiritual blessings in heavenly places in Christ.

Ephesians 3:20

Now unto Him who is able to do exceedingly abundantly above all that we ask or think, according to the power that works in us.

Philippians 4:19

But my God shall supply all your need according to His riches in glory by Christ Jesus.

Colossians 1:12 (brackets added)

Giving thanks to the Father, who has made us meet [worthy] to be partakers of the inheritance of the signs in light.

He qualified us for His best blessings in Christ.

1 Thessalonians 4:12

That you may walk honestly toward those who are without, and that you may have lack of nothing.

2 Thessalonians 3:10

For even when we were with you, this we commanded you, that if any would not work, neither should he eat.

In all labor, or work, there is profit (Proverbs 14:23). God blesses us with work so that we have provision!

1 Timothy 6:17

Charge them who are rich in this world, that they be not highminded, nor trust in uncertain riches, but in the living God, who gives us richly all things to enjoy.

2 Timothy 4:11

*Only Luke is with me. Take Mark, and
bring him with you: for he is profitable to
me for the ministry.*

One way that God prospers us is through relationships. Paul had previously been separated
from Mark over a difference of opinion. Now he
asked for his company as a minister, determin-
ing, that he was profitable for the ministry.

Titus 3:8

*This is a faithful saying, and these things
I will that you affirm constantly, that they
who have believed in God might be care-
ful to maintain good works. These things
are good and profitable to men.*

Living right leads to long-term prosperity.

Philemon 11

*Which in time past was to you
unprofitable, but now profitable to you
and to me.*

Paul encouraged Philemon, a wealthy busi-
nessman and leader in the church, to receive
Onesimus, a runaway servant. Paul wanted to see
the relationship healed and determined that
Onesimus had become profitable to both of them
in terms of the Gospel.

Hebrews 6:13-15

For when God made promise to Abraham, because He could swear by no greater, He swore by Himself, Saying, Surely blessing I will bless you, and multiplying I will multiply you. And so, after he had patiently endured, he obtained the promise.

James 1:25

But whoever looks into the perfect law of liberty, and continues therein, he being not a forgetful hearer, but a doer of the work, this man shall be blessed in his deed.

1 Peter 3:8-10 (brackets added)

Finally, be all of one mind, having compassion one of another, love as brethren, be pitiful, be courteous: Not rendering evil for evil, or railing for railing: but contrariwise blessing; knowing that you are thereunto called, that you should inherit a blessing. For he who will love life, and see good days, let him refrain his tongue from evil, and his lips that they speak no guile [deceit].

2 Peter 1:3

According as His divine power has given us all things that pertain to life and godliness, through the knowledge of Him who called us to glory and virtue.

We have everything we need to do everything God has called us to do. We lack nothing in Christ Jesus.

1 John 3:16-18

> *Hereby perceive we the love of God, because He laid down His life for us: and we ought to lay down our lives for the brethren. But whoever has this world's good, and sees his brother have need, and shuts up his heart of compassion from him, how dwells the love of God in him? My little children, let us not love in word, neither in tongue; but in deed and in truth.*

We not only receive the goodness of God, but we are to share the goodness that He has shared with us.

2 John 4

> *I rejoiced greatly that I found of your children walking in truth, as we have received a commandment from the Father.*

What marvelous provision from God, when our children walk in truth!

3 John 2

> *Beloved, I wish above all things that you may prosper and be in health, even as your soul prospers.*

Jude 20-21

But you, beloved, building up yourselves on your most holy faith, praying in the Holy Ghost, Keep yourselves in the love of God, looking for the mercy of our Lord Jesus Christ unto eternal life.

What blessing we have from God: faith, the Holy Spirit, mercy, love and eternal life. We are blessed by the Most High God, possessor of heaven and earth.

Revelation 21:18-21

And the building of the wall of it was of jasper: and the city was pure gold, like clear glass. And the foundations of the wall of the city were garnished with all manner of precious stones. The first foundation was jasper; the second, sapphire; the third, a chalcedony; the fourth, an emerald; the fifth, a sardonyx; the sixth, sardius; the seventh, chrysolite; the eighth, beryl; the ninth, a topaz; the tenth, a chrysoprasus; the eleventh, a jacinth; the twelfth, an amethyst. And the twelve gates were twelve pearls; every several gate was of one pearl: and the street of the city was pure gold, as it were transparent glass.

Revelation 22:3

And there shall be no more curse: but the throne of God and of the Lamb shall be in it; and his servants shall serve Him.

Not only will the New Jerusalem, the eternal home of believers, be filled with unsurpassed beauty and wealth, there shall be no more curse. It will radiate the blessing of the Almighty!

Yes, there is provision in every book of the Bible!

Chapter

Twenty-Three

PATHWAY TO PROSPERITY

Prosperity is plain and simple in the scripture. Believe the Word of God. Meditate the Word of God. Speak the Word of God and do the Word of God. If you do this, you will make your way prosperous, and you will have good success.

Joshua 1:8

> *This book of the law shall not depart out of your mouth; but you shall meditate therein day and night, so you will observe to do according to all that is written therein: for then you will make your way prosperous, and you will have good success.*

It is paramount that we believe God's Word above everything else. When we give the Word first place in our lives, the Word will bring forth a harvest of life, health, and blessing (Proverbs 4:20-23). For that to happen, we must let the Word have preeminence. The Word of God needs to be our rule of faith, conduct and doctrine. It needs to be our guide in life. When we let the Word rule our lives, we will remain consistent.

The Hebrew word for meditate in Joshua 1:8, and in Psalm 1:1-3, is the Hebrew word *hawgaw*. It means to utter, mutter, think on, ponder, imagine, and dream. When we meditate the Word, the Word changes the picture on the inside of us. When that happens, we can't help but begin to speak differently.

If you see yourself prosperous, you will not continue to talk poverty. You will not be verbalizing lack and need. Your language will change. You will begin to speak words of life and blessing. Death and life are in the power of the tongue. Our words have the ability to change the course of nature (James 3:6).

You cannot grow wealthy by speaking words of lack. Your thinking directs your speaking, and your speaking directs your actions. If you begin to meditate (think on) the Word, if you begin to let the Word of God reprogram the way you think, your words will change. When your thoughts and words change, your action will follow suit.

Believing, meditating on, and speaking the Word of God leads to actions of faith. Faith action produces results. Faith is released through our words and actions. Without faith, it is impossible to please God (Hebrews 11:6). Believing, meditating, speaking, and acting on God's Word will release prosperity and success in life.

Speak God's Word

I am including scriptural confessions that we can make in three areas: provision, healing, and in-Christ realities. Speaking God's Word releases His life into the life of the believer.

Provision

I am blessed and highly favored of the Lord. I am blessed in my body and my mind. I know what to do and how to do it. I have the mind of Christ.

I have plenty of money. I have no lack in any area of my life. I have everything I need to do everything God has called me to do.

My children are blessed. My church is blessed. My home is blessed. My investments are blessed. All of the works of my hands are blessed. I lend, and I do not borrow. My God supplies all of my need according to His riches in glory.

I am prospering financially and physically as my soul prospers. God delights in my prosperity. I do not want. I am a giver. I give to every good work. I abound in the grace of giving. I am reaping an abundant harvest.

The blessing of the Lord overtakes me and makes me rich. I have an abundant supply. I have all sufficiency in all things, and I abound to every good work. I live under an open heaven. God is my provider in every area of my life.

I have so much blessing, I don't have room to contain it. My storehouses are blessed. I have so much abundance, I am an advertisement for how God treats His children.

Blessing overtakes me everywhere I go. Wealth and riches are in my house. The Lord is my help and my shield. The Lord increases me more and more, both me and my children. There is much treasure in my house. I am blessed by the Lord, the possessor of heaven and earth.

I am increasing daily in my knowledge of the Lord, and His blessing is continually overtaking me. Thank God, I am blessed of the Lord, and I am not cursed. Everything I do prospers.

Health

1 Peter 2:24 – By His stripes I was healed.

Isaiah 53:4-5 – He took my pain and carried my sickness. By His stripes I am healed.

Psalm 103:3 – He forgives all of my sins, and He heals all of my diseases.

Exodus 15:26 – He is the Lord my healer.

Psalm 118:17 – I will not die, but I will live and declare the works of the Lord.

Psalm 107:20 – He sent His Word and healed me and delivered me from all my destructions.

Proverbs 4:22 – His Word is life and health to all my flesh.

Psalm 91:10, 16 – No plague comes near my dwelling. With long life He satisfies me and shows me His salvation.

Jeremiah 30:17 – He restores my health and heals my wounds.

Romans 8:11 – The same spirit that raised Christ from the dead is quickening my mortal body.

I am strong and healthy doing the will of God. I live in divine health. I am the healed of the Lord.

In Christ Realities

I am the righteousness of God in Christ. I am sanctified by the blood of Jesus Christ. I am separated to the Gospel of God. I am delivered from every evil word and work.

I am free to be everything God wants me to be. I am complete in Christ. Christ is living in me, moving through me, and strengthening me daily. I am forgiven for every sin.

I am the head and not the tail. I am above only and not beneath. I am blessed with every spiritual blessing in heavenly places in Christ. I am chosen. I am holy and blameless. I am predestined to succeed. I am accepted in the beloved.

I am redeemed from every curse. I have an inheritance that is incorruptible, undefiled, and reserved in heaven for me. I am born of God. I am sealed with the Holy Spirit. I am a citizen of heaven.

I am washed, sanctified, and justified in the name of the Lord Jesus. I am a child of God. The Greater One indwells me. I am victorious through Christ who strengthens me. Christ lives in me. I am more than a conqueror through Him who died for me. I am a new creation in Christ.

Chapter

Twenty-Four

START NOW

Information without application will not help us. We must apply the truth that we know if it is going to change our lives. It is vain to think that we can just keep doing the same things and get different results.

James 2:20

> *But will you know, O vain man, that faith without works is dead?*

We need to begin by examining our belief system. What do we believe about God? What do we believe about ourselves? How do we see life?

Do we believe that God is good and that He wants us to prosper? If we don't, we need to examine our beliefs in light of the scriptures.

Do we believe that we have gifts and talents from God and that we have the ability to prosper? Do we see opportunity, or do we see opposition?

Winston Churchill said, "A pessimist sees the difficulty in every opportunity. An optimist sees the opportunity in every difficulty."

If we can see the opportunity, we might just realize it!

Do we have a long-term plan to prosper? Are we operating in the 10/10/80 plan? What churches or ministries are we allocating at least 10% of our income to? If you are the decision maker for a ministry or church, ask yourself this same question about the ministry or church you steward.

What vehicles do we have in place for saving at least 10% of our income? Savings accounts, investment accounts, extra principal payments on a house, increasing equity in businesses that are equitable and profitable, and retirement accounts may be some viable options.

Have we balanced our budget? Are we committed to living within our means? Are we believing to eliminate debt, or better yet, to substantially increase our net worth? Do we have practical plans in place to do it?

A good friend of mine says, "Boys make excuses while men make decisions." Make a decision to believe God. Make a decision to move into what He has for you. Make a decision to prosper.

Apply the truth that you know. God is not obligated to give us more revelation until we act on the revelation that He has already given us. Have we done the last thing God told us to do?

Several times in my life I have made the inward decision to never let money be the primary reason for my choices, but to completely obey God.

When I was 17 years old, just after my father had passed away, my grandparents made me an offer to give me their ranch. The condition was that I would run it myself. I turned the offer down because I knew that God had called me to preach, and I knew that I might not be able to run that ranch and completely obey God.

When I was pastoring in Kit Carson, one of my mentors bought several sections of land. He offered to let me buy one of them. (A section is a square mile: 640 acres). I went and looked at it, and I knew it would make money.

However, God said, "No." No means no. So, I obeyed. Money is not my primary motivation. Faith in God is my primary motivation. Money is simply a biproduct of my relationship with God.

I seek to never violate my relationship with God. I want to obey Him completely and explicitly! He is my life. He is my hope. He is my reward!

Obeying God has ultimately led to increased blessing in my life.

Some of our greatest opportunities are followed by accepting some of our greatest challenges. One of the hardest decisions that I ever made was the decision to move to Colorado Springs and start Charis Christian Center. Initially, it was very challenging, but it has also been one of the most rewarding things in my life.

At the bottom of the economic downturn in real estate in the United States in 2011, Barbara and I purchased a home. It was initially very challenging to do; I had to go to several banks before I found one who would loan us the money. However, in the end, it has been a great financial blessing!

When Charis Christian Center bought the property at 10285 Federal Drive in Colorado Springs, it really stretched me. We went from paying $1,000 per month in utilities to paying $10,000 a month in utilities! The larger building takes more money to operate, and it requires more staff. But it also gives us the opportunity to reach more people and to help more ministries.

I know this is not the end, but just a step in the plan that God has for us. If we are going to totally obey God, we must do it one step at a time, one day at a time. The end of a thing is better than the beginning.

But to get to the end, you must begin.

RECEIVE JESUS

If you have never received Jesus Christ as your personal Lord and Savior, I invite you to receive Him now. The best decision I have ever made in my life is to receive Jesus Christ as my Savior and to surrender to Him as Lord.

Jesus has been really good to me, and He is no respecter of persons. Jesus will be good to you as well if you let Him.

Romans 10:8-10 declares, *"The Word is near you, in your mouth and in your heart" (that is, the word of faith that we preach): that if you confess with your mouth the Lord Jesus and believe in your heart that God has raised Him from the dead, you will be saved. For with the heart one believes unto righteousness, and with the mouth confession is made unto salvation"* (NKJV).

Jesus, the Son of God, came to earth. He lived a sinless, holy, perfect, and pure life. Yet, He died on the cross, taking our sins. He was buried for three days, and God raised Him from the dead, making Him Lord of all. The work has already been done for your salvation; all you need to do is believe it and receive Jesus. Just pray this prayer for yourself:

God, I believe Jesus Christ is Your Son. I believe Jesus died for my sins. I believe that You raised Him from the dead and made Him Lord. Jesus, right now, I receive Your forgiveness for my sins, and I confess You as my Lord. I ask You to come live Your life in me. I will live for You as You give me the strength. In the Name of Jesus, I pray. Amen.

If you prayed that prayer, and meant it from your heart, Jesus is now your Lord. You are on your way to heaven. Welcome to the family!

Going forward, I suggest that you get a Bible and read some every day. I would begin in the New Testament. I also suggest that you talk to God—pray every day. Listen to hear His voice speaking to you.

I would also ask that you find a good Bible-teaching church where Jesus is exalted. Last, but not least, tell someone that you know loves Jesus about your decision, and find some Bible-believing, Jesus-loving friends to enjoy life with. Blessings await you as you walk with Jesus!

Made in the USA
Monee, IL
24 November 2021